TRAMP
after God

TRAMP
after God

Willie Mullan
with Gladys and Derrick Knowlton

MARSHALL, MORGAN & SCOTT

LAKELAND
Marshall, Morgan & Scott
a Pentos company
1 Bath Street, London EC1V 9LB

© Gladys and Derrick Knowlton 1979
First published 1979
Reprinted
Impression number 10 9 8 7 6 5 4 3

ISBN 0 551 00811 3

Printed in Great Britain by
Hunt Barnard Printing Ltd., Aylesbury, Bucks

In memory of Gladys who died after writing
the first half of this book. Her inspiration
enabled her husband to complete it.

Man is born to live not
to prepare for life.
(Boris Pasternak)

Contents

1: Barefoot boy

The tall soldier stooped to lift me in firm hands, swinging me up in a dizzying arc and holding me suspended at arm's length above him. I squealed with half-fearful delight as I looked down – a long way, it seemed – into his laughing, upturned face; then he set me down and took his place by the troops. He was the Sergeant Major, and he was my father, and that brief contact was the last I ever saw of him.

There were a lot of soldiers in the town that day, closely packed, dense columns of them, marching to Belfast. To me, a wee boy, the fact that the Royal Ulster Rifles were going to war meant little; until my father came along I had been absorbed in staring wide-eyed at the grand-looking officer who rode a big white horse at the head of his men.

Ahead lay the fighting, and on 1st June, 1916, when I was five years old, my father was killed at the Battle of the Somme. My mother was left a widow with no pension until later, owing to an official mix-up, and with seventeen children to feed and clothe in the small house at Newtownards, Northern Ireland, that was our home.

Yes, I was the youngest of seventeen! Sixteen of us were boys and the eldest, Lizzie, was a girl. To me she was another mother-figure, someone in authority who wouldn't think twice about beating you or boxing your ears if you misbehaved. I used to keep out of her way whenever it seemed prudent!

Mother worked valiantly to keep the home going after Father died. She was just a little woman in a skirt and shawl, but in addition to all her work at home she was soon tackling jobs like washing floors in offices and pubs in the early mornings and laundering shirts for the gentry to earn a shilling or two.

Mother's name was Mary, a beautiful, gentle name. There was nothing gentle, though, about the way she kept the lot of us in order. She ruled her family with iron discipline and from the big boys to the youngest we all jumped to obey her orders. She had a powerful voice, and she had no hesitation in giving us a whack with anything handy to enforce our obedience.

So there we were, poor and fatherless in an overcrowded house. Yet I remember those childhood years as among my happiest times. For all Mother's strictness we loved her and knew she loved us, every one, and our evenings, with the day's work and schooling done, were contented and full of fun.

Mealtimes were all-important to a growing lad! Mother had a big black cooking-pot full of potatoes, scrubbed and boiled in their skins, which hung over the fire. When they were cooked, the skins cracked and insides softened to a lovely floury whiteness, she would strain them and tip the lot onto the bare kitchen table for us to help ourselves. There was always a jug of buttermilk – I used to fetch it from the farm two miles away, where it was given free for the asking – and with our plates and mugs my brothers and I would sit down, just anywhere, on the uneven, red-tiled floor. We had no carpets and our feet were bare; I went barefoot all my young days and was as tough and lively as a young animal, firm-limbed and rosy-faced, with strong white teeth and clear eyes.

There was something to be done before we could start our simple meal.

'Quiet now,' Mother would hold up a hand. Then: 'Lord, we thank you for this good food and ask your blessing upon it,' she would say. Our 'Amen' was the signal to start, and believe me, we needed no second bidding!

After tea we really enjoyed ourselves. We had no television, true enough, but we made our own entertainment. 'Give us a tune Tom,' someone would beg, and my big brother Tom would fetch his accordion whilst another brother, George, brought out his flute. Then the older boys would begin to sing the old Irish ballads such as 'The stone outside Dan

Murphy's door' and 'The bold Philim Brady, the bard of Armagh,' with the rest of us joining in.

Presently Mother would look up from her sewing in the big armchair under the oil-lamp.

'Now then boys, make room for Wee Hugh . . . ' and we would scramble to one side, faces shining with pleasure, so that Hugh could do a stepdance, his feet tapping with a captivating rhythm. Hugh was much in demand at socials and parties and concerts all over the country, so you can tell he could really stepdance well.

The fun went on all evening, and I think that being the youngest I had the most fun of them all. Mother kept order with an occasional 'Now, now . . . ' until at ten o'clock she would decree, 'Bedtime, boys,' and bring the party to an end.

Now, more than half a century later, I can remember as clearly the scene which always followed. In my mind's eye I can see that shabby room and the seventeen of us kneeling down, keeping perfectly still while Mother prayed, her eyes lifted to Heaven. Her grateful thanks to God for all his mercies invariably came first, humble and sincere. Then she would pray for us each in turn, Lizzie, Tom, Hugh . . . until she came to me, the youngest. I'm afraid I often wished she would hurry up and get to me so the session would be over, and sometimes I was naughty enough to lift my own eyes and watch her, growing restless if I thought she was praying too long over one of the others.

When my turn came she always ended her prayers like this: 'Dear Lord, bless Willie; save him one day and make him a man of God.' Those words came from a mother's heart, day after day, year after year, and God heard them, yes, and answered.

The older boys might go out for a bit after prayer time, but we younger ones trooped up to our bedroom. More of a loft it was really, with no ceiling between us and the rafters and some gaping holes in the roof where the rain could get in. Six to a bed we were, top and bottom, all faces and feet and just a candle for light. Then, when we were all snug and the candle blown out, Wee Hugh would start his mischief.

'Once upon a time there was a big, big, white ghost . . . '

Hugh's voice was weird and spooky in the darkness. Then he would reach out and grab one of us by the leg with blood-curdling moans and strange noises until we screamed with delighted mock-terror which gave way to laughter. Soon, though, Mother's voice would call up, 'Quiet! Get to sleep, now.' Then sleep would come, deep sleep, blessed sleep, until the same voice woke us to another day.

Of course we had no such thing as a bathroom. Summer and winter we washed in cold water, sharing two old tin basins and a couple of towels between the tribe of us. All the same we had to pass an inspection by Mother or Lizzie of our faces, hands, ears, neck and feet before we were allowed out to school.

Breakfast always consisted of two slices of bread and margarine – and you should just see how quickly a quarter-pound of marg. could vanish with seventeen knives all dabbing at it together!

The baking of our bread became my job when I was about eleven. We all had our tasks to do; the big table had to be scrubbed white as snow every day, the uncarpeted stairs and the tiled floor washed, and so on. My work, as soon as I got home from school, was to bake the bread – soda bread, wheaten bread, potato bread, oat cake ... I got to be quite an expert, and you can guess how much was consumed every day by a hungry family of boys. Still, I was proud of my cooking and liked to think that the big griddle, the baking board and bowl, bag of flour, bird's wing duster and all the rest of it were in my sole charge. The griddle hung on a chain over the open fire, and many a good oat cake did I produce on its heat.

Two slices of bread and marg. again for our school lunch, rolled up in newspaper with our school books, and since our school had neither dinners nor dining-hall we ate our food in the yard all year round.

This yard was covered with 'screening' from the local quarry – little blue stone chippings which were very hard on our bare feet. We soon got use to it, though, and some of us barefoot scholars could soon run faster than the 'toffs' who wore shoes; yes, and we played football barefoot, too. I could meet that ball with my unshielded toes and give it a kick which would send it flying, and never feel a thing.

Football was a favourite sport with me, in fact, and I was often out with the lads playing in the street on a summer's evening.

'Get in! Get in! The mail's coming!' That was the cry which went up when at six o'clock the Royal Mail van – the first motor vehicle I ever saw – came ponderously along the street. It travelled at about five miles an hour, I should think! But to us the sight was an exciting one as we cowered back by the wall clutching our precious ball.

We had a football team at school, and after a while I was made its captain. How proud I was! We had won several cups and the schoolmaster liked us to be well turned out, particularly, it appeared, for one special game which was in prospect.

'This is a very important occasion, boys,' he told us. 'You will all get new jerseys and pants from the school, and I want you all to get a pair of new boots.'

My heart went right down to my feet. What chance did I have of buying new boots? Happy to be barefoot, the most I could muster was an ancient pair of handed-down, very grubby boots. I put the problem to Mother, but I already knew the answer.

'I fear you've no chance at all Willie, the way things are with us.' The touch of sympathy in her voice did nothing to ease my sore heart, and I had to fight back the tears.

Then an amazing thing happened. Right on the very day before the match I saw Mother coming home from work, and there hung on her shawl was a fine new pair of football boots; I knew at once they were just my size.

Somehow she had managed to put aside a penny here, another there, so that this youngest son of hers should not be disgraced before the school. That was how she loved us, this hard-working, God-fearing little woman. I am glad to say we won the match; it was a day of glory for young Willie Mullan, I can tell you!

Now you would have expected that this good mother, who so loved the Lord herself, would have sent all us children to Sunday school. Well you'd have been right, but I have to report that I never got there. Oh, I would start off all right, but it was a long walk and there would be all sorts of interesting things to divert me on the way. For instance, there was the day I went to the forest.

That was an unusual sort of day, for I actually had a new coat. Mostly, being the youngest, I had to be content with clothes of all sorts and sizes, passed down the family till they reached me in a pretty worn-out state. This time, though, I had a new jacket – but that didn't stop me joining the other boys when one suggested spending Sunday afternoon in the forest climbing a few trees. We weren't in the least troubled in our conscience about missing Sunday school yet again; we called it mitching and it was a regular occurrence.

Well, so there was young Willie Mullan, scrambling up the trees, as happy as any monkey – until it was time to climb back down. Then, oh dear, oh dear, I made a bad job of it; I slipped and came down in a rush, catching my new jacket on a branch and ripping the back of it nearly out.

'W . . . what will I say to Mother?' I wanted to know.

My companions were no help. 'She'll kill you, that's for sure,' was the general verdict, and they were very nearly right! I hung about for a long time, afraid to go home, but at last I had to face my mother's righteous anger. My, I can tell you I was pretty sore for a few days. Would you believe it, though, by the next week I was mitching Sunday school again?

The day school I attended changed its name several times. First it was the Church School, then it became the National and lastly the Public Elementary School, but whatever its name I hated many of the lessons it tried to teach me. I did love the sports, as I have said, and I enjoyed history and geography. Religious instruction, too, was a favourite, and I listened spellbound to the Bible stories, although I questioned the reality of God in my mind and had none of the simple faith of my dear old mother. But as for the other lessons, well, I couldn't spell and I couldn't add up, and I was constantly in trouble. In my last years at school I got caned every day, and sometimes the Headmaster would lose patience with me when I would not flinch, and he would whack me round the legs. I had started off all right with a lady teacher who took

14

pains with me, but in those later years I became more and more stubborn and unruly, throwing my slates at the teacher and causing an uproar on many days.

I am truly sorry now that I was such a nuisance and so stupid. Our old Headmaster was a great soul who had an almost impossible task. Actually I had a secret respect for him, even on my worst days, but he never knew it.

Still, I was happy out of school, and had one plaything, a big iron hoop given me by a blacksmith. Miles and miles I would run after that hoop, one of a group of perhaps ten boys, our bare feet keeping pace on stones and dust and mud with barely a pause for breath. When we got hungry we might take a turnip from a farmer's field; we would split it in half on the top of a gate and eat it raw, crunching it with real enjoyment. Happy days indeed!

So the years went by until I was counting the days until I left school. I completed my education in the fourth standard of the Public Elementary, and God alone knows how I got that far. One Friday I left, to begin my working life on the following Monday. A new stage had been reached, and an important one for me.

How proud I was to be starting work! I had got a job driving a milk cart on a round, and every day I was up with the lark, hurrying round to the stable to groom the horse and harness him to the cart. I soon learned all the parts of his harness, the bridle, collar, hems, backband, traces and so on, and greatly admired the lovely old cart with its two big shining polished milk-cans, covered in summer with snow-white linen coverings.

All round the town I drove, measuring out pints and half-pints for my customers. One of them was the Headmaster's wife and one day she had a word with me.

'I'm very glad to see you're settling down Willie and working so well,' she told me. I had a good idea, mind, why she was glad I was no longer a schoolboy; the place must have been a lot more peaceful without me!

In the evenings I had another job, this time selling news-papers, the Belfast Telegraph, Newtownards Chronicle and the Bangor Spectacle, at my pitch near the railway station.

I was one of a gang of newsboys. I can see us now, clustered round the delivery man, collecting our bundles of papers, all of us clad in dark jerseys and caps, knickerbockers buttoned at the knee, and every one of us barefoot in rain, hail, snow or frost. Our feet were used to the elements and we thought it no hardship, but some of the boys were often hungry and some indeed half starving.

One day in particular comes to memory now. One of the lads was a lad called Little Glendinning; his mother was a kindly soul who would sometimes give me a piece of bread and jam when I called at her door. Well on this occasion Little Glendinning had just that – a piece of bread and jam. He was just about to eat it when up came a big dog, Hector, who we knew to be as hungry as we often were; he would snatch anything that looked eatable.

Of course Little Glendinning wasn't going to lose his precious snack, so he slipped it up inside his jersey, quick as a flash, jam side against his belly, and eventually Hector made off. Then out came the bread and jam, and Glendinning began to tuck in – and that was when a little fellow, a thin, hungry waif of a child, crept up and licked the bits of jam off his belly where they had stuck. Yes, there were boys who knew what hunger was in those days, sure enough.

Some days, though, we had a windfall, like the time when a man gave me sixpence for a penny paper and told me to keep the change. You could buy a dozen Paris buns, full of currants, for threepence at the baker's shop, and the man always gave you thirteen. Tucking in to those we were as happy as lords, I can tell you. I became a super salesman with my papers, earning a halfpenny per dozen, but of course I gave all my actual earnings to Mother, only keeping any 'tips' for myself.

I still had another job to do before the day was done. Back to the dairy I would go, and with the milk cart and horse (though without the big cans) I made my way each evening to the big camp where thousands of soldiers were stationed. My job was to remove the swill barrels from the cookhouse and deliver their contents to a farmer who kept pigs. I liked the job and got on well with the Regimental Sergeant Major, a big, bluff man who would come and have a word with me.

'Come here and let me feel those cold feet.' He could scarce believe I didn't feel the cold as I jumped down from the cart into the snow. 'My, you are a brave youngster and no mistake. Here, bring the swill barrel; I've got a bit of meat your mother can use, I daresay . . . ' He would fetch a side of bacon or a big roast joint and drop it into the barrel among all the greasy soup and tealeaves and other leftovers.

'The guard on the gate won't find it, Willie' When you get home, take it out before you go on to the farmer and tell your mother if she washes it well it will be quite good to eat.'

He was a good fellow; he knew my mother was a widow and struggling to make ends meet, so he tried to help, and many a night we feasted on pork ribs or roast beef – though I have to admit it was at the government's expense.

Well, a couple of years went by with me working hard and enjoying life. My older brothers had jobs too, and most of them did very well in later years, so it seemed Mother's burdens had lifted. Then a terrible thing happened to me.

It began with a casual meeting in the street. Two fellows I knew stopped to tell me they'd had a win on the horse they had backed, and I thought I could add to their good fortune.

'You'll be on a winning streak, sure enough,' I told them. 'Now what you should do is to put it all on another horse; then you'll *really* have some winnings.'

And would you believe it, they did that, and do you know, the horse won! Those two men could scarcely believe their luck.

'Sure, we owe it all to you, Willie lad,' one of them said. 'Come on down to the pub and we'll buy you a drink.'

Well I was just a boy of sixteen and I felt mighty grown-up to be strolling into that pub and taking my very first glass of beer. This was a man's life all right, I was sure.

But those two men did something to me that altered my whole life. You see that glass led to another, and another . . . and by the time I left the pub I was not only drunk (though that was bad enough) but also addicted to drink.

It was quite late when I staggered along our street. For a moment I held on to the wall of our house, fumbling for the door; then I got it open and fell inside.

I had missed Mother's prayer time that night, that was certain. My brother Tom was waiting, though, just inside the door.

'Why you filthy young rebel, you're drunk!' His voice held anger as well as surprise, and quick as a flash his big fist sent me sprawling, head over heels, with a powerful blow.

The room reeled around me, but I became dizzily aware of hasty footsteps and someone bending over me. It was Mother.

'Leave him alone! You've no right to hit him; he's mine. Oh Willie, Willie . . .'

Very tenderly she helped me onto the couch and put a rug over me. Then, as my brother turned away, Mother knelt beside me and poured out her heart in anguished prayer.

That scene was to be repeated night after night for many weeks. Every evening now found me at the pub, and although I had no money I had enough brains to know that I could talk a bit and sing a bit and soon enough someone would buy me a drink or two . . .

Mother soon realised I was completely 'hooked' on drink.

'Dear Lord,' she prayed over and over, 'he is in the grip of this thing. Oh, won't you set him free?' And her words hit me far harder than my brother ever did, I can tell you.

The thing was, I didn't even *like* the stuff I was drinking now. Often I hated it. But I was in an iron grip, and although I didn't know it then I was never to come home sober from that day when I was sixteen until I was twenty-four. I lost my jobs, I became known all round the neighbourhood as the black sheep of the family, yet I just could not leave the drink alone.

One day, still in my seventeenth year, something even more dreadful happened. I was in the house alone with Mother – I suppose all the others were away at work – when I happened to notice her face.

Something was twisting her features. She was having some sort of seizure. Alarmed, I gripped her shoulders and eased her onto the couch, at a loss what to do next.

Suddenly she began to breathe heavily; then she turned her face up towards Heaven and her lips moved faintly.

There was one deep sigh . . . and then silence. Mother was dead, as suddenly as that.

Now I thought my heart would break. You see, I had none of Mother's faith to believe she had gone to be with the Lord, which the Bible tells us is far better. I just knew I had lost the best friend I ever had at that moment, for I realised that whatever I did or however badly I behaved she had always gone on loving me and praying for me, 'Lord, bless Willie; save him and make him a man of God someday.' Even now I was a drunkard her love had never failed, and neither had her hope in me.

Well then there was the wake, with all the neighbours and friends coming in to pay their respects, and do you know I disgraced myself again by going off and getting drunk, thinking to drown my sorrows. Just before the undertaker came to take Mother's body away I went into the little room where the coffin lay, shutting the door behind me.

I no longer felt myself to be a big man. Now I was just a lad again, meeting for the first time the utter coldness and stillness of a loved one's dead body. In an agony of remorse and grief I cried, 'Mummy, I promise you I'll never be drunk again,' and I meant it with all my heart. Yet within a couple of hours I was full of the stuff, incapable and stupid. I was bound by shackles that I could not break, however hard I tried.

When the funeral was over the time came when my brothers had to decide what was to be done with Mother's things – and me. Some of them were married now, and Tom turned to one of them and asked, 'What's to be done with Willie? Will you give him a home from now on?'

'Oh no, I couldn't. I've got children of my own to think of now. What sort of an example would a drunken lout like Willie set them?'

'Well then, will *you* take him?'

I kept my head down so as not to see which brother was being addressed, but I heard the answer clearly enough.

'Not me. I could never manage him. He must go with one of the others.'

I could see nobody wanted me and in spite of my misery

19

I couldn't find it in my heart to blame them. They were all hard-working, honest men with decent homes. What would they do with a character like me around the place?

There in that room I knew my way was to be a lonely one. Something in my nature, the old stubbornness I had shown at school, rose to the surface, and I squared my shoulders.

'It's all right; you just go back to your homes and I hope you all do well. I'll look after myself from now on.' With a proud gesture I lifted my coat from behind the door and put it over my arm. Then I walked out, into the night.

2: Alone

Of course the first place I made for was the pub. There was a drink I was taken with which was called tony wine. Strong stuff it was, rough and so potent that half a bottle would make a man incapable. A bottle held ten glassfuls and cost one shilling and sixpence. Well, I laid out my money that evening and pocketed my bottle of tony. I had just one shilling left in the world, nothing else but the clothes I stood up in, and I was barely seventeen. My life as a tramp had just begun.

I walked out of the town for about five miles and around midnight I climbed over a gate at the entrance to a plantation of trees. In the dark I picked my way through the tree trunks, my ears keen to the small sounds of birds stirring in the branches as I passed. I found a sheltered spot at the base of a tree, lay down, and propping myself on one elbow began to drink my tony wine. I had no fear of the dark; I had a long knife and I drew it out of my belt, sticking it in the ground as a safeguard. Now I felt at ease to drink at leisure, thinking my silent thoughts. Mother's death was still fresh in my mind, but I began telling myself that maybe there was no God up there; no heaven or hell, no hereafter, only this life and a drink inside a man . . . I tipped up the bottle and soon had finished nearly all its contents.

When I awoke the dawn light was filtering its way through the trees. I walked down to a stream, washed my face and dried it with my shirt. I wore no underclothes and the damp shirt soon dried on my skin; I had no fear of cold and in fact felt a great confidence and cheerfulness. I'd get along just fine; I'd show them all. I whistled as I climbed back onto the road.

I little knew then that with the new day I had started on a new way of life. Three and a half years were to pass before

21

I slept in a bed again, three and a half years of summers and winters, of storms and blazing sun, of snow and frost and torrential rain. Night after night of sleeping in fields and barns and empty buildings, in cowsheds and on railway embankments. Day after day of walking, begging for food, sometimes picking up a casual labouring job for a while, days of going without food (once I ate nothing for four whole days) – but never, never a day that ended without me getting drunk. Somehow, if I had to beg it or spend my last copper, I got my bottle each evening, and with that I was content.

As I stepped out on this new day I caught up with a farmer driving some cattle.

'Can I help you at all?' I called. 'I'm looking for a job.'

'That you can. I'll give you five bob and your food for a day's work.'

So I found my first casual job. At eight o'clock that evening I went down to the village pub and bought my usual tony wine, but this time the barman looked at me keenly.

'You know son, if you keep drinking that monkey's blood the devil will get you early.' It was a kindly warning and well meant, but I paid no heed; soon I was finding a place to sleep under a hedge and eagerly uncorking my bottle.

So the summer passed, and all too soon the cold rains of autumn were drifting across the country; the rains drawn by the mountains of Ireland, rains that went on and on for days. Often I was soaked through and through, and would just gurgle as much tony wine as I could so that I could sleep in my wet clothes without too much discomfort. I was a real tramp now, with no one to care if I had a bed or food or decent clothing. At first my family had tried to help me pull myself together. My sister found out where I was and bought me a brand new suit – but I only sold it or pawned it, I forget which, and used the money to buy more drink. There was nothing any of them could do for me now.

Sometimes I looked for shelter at night, and one night I had a hair-raising experience. I had discovered an old disused house in the country. It had no doors or windows and it seemed the farmer had used it for sawing logs, since a number of tree roots were lying about. In the corner was some straw, so I had my bed booked for the night and was feeling rather cheery as I made my way there, rather the worse for drink, about midnight.

The night was very dark. A storm was raging, the wind at gale force and the rain lashing down on the tumbledown roof. But I was not worried. I felt my way to the straw and was just about to lie down and open my bottle when I saw two shining eyes close by me, three times as large as cats' eyes and about three feet from the ground. My, I sobered up pretty quickly, I can tell you!

Now there was just one question in my mind– what *was* this creature? Was it a wild beast escaped from captivity? Those huge eyes never moved, never flickered. Was it a terrible demon, an unearthly thing? I knew I could hold my own with man or beast with a knife in my hand, but the unwinking stillness of those huge eyes made the hair on the back of my neck stand up. I was terrified.

Something had to be done; it was between me and the door. For a moment I listened in the dark. No breathing, no bark, no growl . . . I inched forward, my knife held ready, and picked up a stone from the floor with my left hand.

'Get out! I have a knife and I'll not hesitate to use it. Get out!' The sweat ran from me as I shouted the words into the silence. Nothing moved.

Suddenly I threw the stone right between those eyes, plunging my knife after it. Then I moved to examine my prey, putting out my hand to feel its shape.

It was the root of a tree, and the two 'eyes' were patches of phosphorescence. I could have sobbed with relief. In a matter of moments I was gulping my drink, eager for oblivion. What a night that was!

Another time I made room for myself by turning the rightful owners out of a cattle shed! The poor beasts bellowed a bit, but they moved off into the cold field and I bedded down on a pile of hay.

In the early hours the door creaked open and I saw the figure of a man outlined against the sky. He came in, quietly shutting the door.

I spoke quietly into the darkness. 'Who are you? I'm

warning you, I have a knife and I can use it. Speak up now, what is it you're wanting?'

The man was plainly terrified. 'I swear I didn't know anyone was here. Sure, all I'm after is a bit of shelter and a sleep.'

I moved over on the hay. 'Lie down then with your back to me. And if I get the smallest hint of trouble from you, this knife is in you quicker than your next breath.'

I felt the hay yield under his weight, then there was silence. I dared not sleep lest he steal my knife, or worse, attack me, and I'm sure that the poor fellow got never a wink of sleep either. We just lay there wakeful and tense, two people in desperate straights yet afraid to trust each other. When the first streaks of dawn came I said, 'Right; clear out now,' and I can tell you he went with never a backward look.

People sometimes use the expression 'honour among thieves,' and perhaps there is a sort of loyalty when felons stick together to save their necks. Ah, but there can be a terrible mistrust, too, among vagabonds, and a fierce concern for one's own safety which makes every man an enemy at times. It is the very opposite of Christ's love – but of course I didn't realise that just then. I only knew I was glad to be rid of my unwelcome companion as stiff and weary I got up to face another day.

Well somehow I got through that winter and presently it was summer again. For a while I got a job at a famous rose-growing nursery, tying in buds. The man I worked with was one of the fastest rose budders that ever lived; he could bud a thousand roses with ease in one day. We worked long hours, from seven a.m. to eight-thirty p.m. and my pay was under ten shillings a week, but however tired I was I always got to the pub at night for my tony wine. With two other casual labourers I slept in the rose field every night for six weeks, eating bread and marg. for breakfast and boiling up potatoes in an old bucket for lunch, with tea and tony to drink. I could have stayed on at that job, but no, I was a wanderer by now and after a bit I moved on, helping farmers with the hay and digging the potato harvest.

That was hard work sure enough, potato harvesting went on from dawn till dark, and my, how your back would ache by then! I was never too worn out, though, to find my way to the nearest pub and drink away the rest of the evening.

One day I felt more than usually weary. Aching pains began weighing down my limbs, my chest hurt and a sweat broke out all over me. In all my life I had scarcely ever been ill, even when exposed to the icy weather of the previous winter. Now, though, I felt desperately unwell and I stumbled off to a far corner of the field and just lay down between the plant-rows, utterly wretched.

I lost count of the days as I lay in that uncomfortable spot. Hour after hour I sweated and suffered, yet somehow I never failed to hobble to the pub each night for my bottle of drink and the poor comfort it offered.

After some days the wracking pain subsided and I got slowly better; eventually I forgot all about the whole painful episode. Years later though I had some chest X-rays and the doctor looked at the plates with some surprise.

'You seem to be an extremely healthy man. How did you come to get these two great scars on your lungs? You had double pneumonia at sometime, sure enough.'

Then I remembered the potato field where I had lain and suffered.

'Ah well,' I said, 'it was a long time ago, sure it was.'

That potato harvest was completed at last. The winter which followed was one of the worst in living memory. I tramped from place to place, and often was almost beat with the icy weather. One day I made my way back to the nursery where I had worked and sought out the foreman.

'Could you give me some sort of shelter just for a few nights, sir?' I asked. He eyed me with sympathy for he was a kindly man.

'Well Willie, there is the stoke hole. You know the boiler is on all night for heating the greenhouses. You can sleep on the layer of sand on top of the boiler.'

So that night found me going down the steps into the stoke hole. There was water on the floor but I quickly clambered up onto the boiler and found my way in the darkness to the six inches of warm sand which covered its top. It was like an electric blanket; I thought I had discovered paradise! I lay

25

down and drank half a bottle of tony, planning to hibernate here each night through the winter, and I drifted off to sleep as happy as a lord.

Alas, there was a drawback to this heaven. Somewhere around three o'clock I woke suddenly. Something was burning; I could smell scorching. It was my clothes; the sand was burning hot and they were already smouldering. I had to get down, and quickly.

Now I was in a fix. Outside it was snowing hard and still dark. On the floor was a layer of cold water, so I couldn't lie there. I began to feel around the walls and at last I found a box propped against one of them. There, cramped and uncomfortable, I spent the rest of the night.

So that night turned out to be a bad one, but there was a far, far worse one to come. It happened in the depth of winter, on the coldest night I had ever known.

That night I had no hospitable shelter. I had been drinking hard and was too befuddled to care or even to realise what a hard frost was settling on the land. I found a railway embankment, lurched down it and was soon asleep.

It was the first train, passing at four-thirty in the morning, which woke me, and I truly believe that train saved my life. For when I came to my senses I found I was literally frozen stiff; I couldn't move my arms or legs and even my fingers would scarcely respond to my efforts to flex them. I lay there like a dead thing and tried to think coherently.

I knew I had to work hard if I was ever to bring my circulation back. Gradually, agonisingly, I started making feeble movements with my hands until I was rubbing my arms and then my legs, dragging my lifeless hands over flesh that had lost every scrap of feeling. The cruel, hard frost had numbed my every nerve.

A whole hour later, when the five-thirty train went by, I was still there, dragging my reluctant hands up and down, up and down, over my frozen limbs. A whole hour! I can tell you, I nearly gave up that morning and let myself die on that railway embankment.

Some instinct for self-preservation kept me going, though,

and at last, nearly exhausted, I crawled up the bank to a nearby cottage.

An old woman was starting her morning chores; at first she seemed scared by my arrival.

'Can you help me – I'm dead beat,' I got out.

That good soul took one look at me, then she helped me inside and gave me a bowl of nourishing, warm soup. Oh, that soup put the life back into me; to this day I am grateful at the remembrance of her kindness.

After that I knew I would have to sleep under some sort of shelter in the future. Fortunately I knew of some premises owned by a large business concern. They were surrounded by a wall, but once over that I could find a shed where there was a lot of packing material, bags and shavings and the like, just right for a good bed. I soon got to know the movements of the nightwatchman, and I would wait till he had passed the shed on his midnight rounds before slipping inside to sleep soundly till five, when I had to get out before the early workers came and spotted me.

One morning I left my shed and walked about a mile down the road to a lake. I washed my face with a bit of soap I carried in my pocket, drank a quarter-bottle of wine and ate a bit of bread. Breakfast was over.

On the way back I was about to pass the wall over which I had climbed when I noticed three policemen examining a certain spot. Something was wrong; I walked on quickly and disappeared from the immediate neighbourhood. I would come back at ten o'clock, I decided, since that was when the pubs opened and I could get some news.

I did hear some news, and I didn't like it at all. The firm had been broken into and about a thousand pounds had been stolen. I was in trouble, for my footprints were all over the wall and on the shed floor, and there was even worse evidence against me. I learned that the thief had cut his hand in smashing a window and there was blood on the sill. Well, I had bought myself a tin of pears recently and had cut my hand trying to open it with my knife. There was the wound for all to see. Now I knew all about circumstantial evidence; why, the case was loaded against me.

Well, I went to another pub where the 'bad boys' hung out, and I listened carefully. There was plenty of talk and that thousand pounds was soon multiplied by twenty, but I learned nothing to help me and I expected every minute to be arrested. Then, late in the morning, a man came in.

Somehow I knew at once that he was the thief. He laughed and joked, and bought all his pals a drink, and then he saw me.

'And who's this then? Like a drink, lad? Been sleeping out, have you? In a certain place, perhaps?'

His eyes narrowed. 'Cut your hand, too. Well, well. You know if I were you I should go round to the police station and plead guilty to that little job last night. Don't try to argue with anyone, you just plead guilty; that way you'll get a lighter sentence, maybe. They'll be taking you in for questioning soon, that's for sure, so drink up while you can.' He gave me three pounds, and I knew it was meant to keep me there while he nipped round and reported me to the police.

He decided to order his pals one more drink first, though, and that was where I stole a march on the rogue. Slipping out quietly, I made straight for the police station myself.

My wandering ways were well known to the officer in charge. He eyed me keenly over his desk.

'Well, Willie, are you in trouble, now?'

His tone invited confidence and soon I was pouring out the whole tale, omitting nothing. When I finished he stood up.

'Say no more, Willie; you can clear off.' He called to a detective and ordered him to go to the pub and arrest such-and-such a man; it appeared my villain had a reputation too. It ended with the rogue being caught and the money restored, but as for me, I had been as near as I liked to think about to a prison cell, and I decided to leave the district right away. I knew where I was bound for. I would go back to my old home town.

3: The den

All the morning's activities were well under way when I walked through the main street of the town I knew so well. Women pushing prams on their way to the shops, children on errands, people everywhere, all with their own concerns. I shuffled along, a bearded figure in ragged clothes and worn-out shoes, and nobody paid any heed to me at all.

Two young fellows who had been my schoolmates came towards me, talking easily together. I paused and almost put out a hand, but after one startled glance they hurried on, not recognising me or not wanting to acknowledge the disreputable creature I had now become.

The scene was repeated all down the street. People I had once known stared and turned sharply away or walked quickly past pretending I did not exist. It was not a pleasant experience at all, I can tell you, and after I had taken as much as I could stand I turned into a side alley to escape the crowds.

It was a tumbledown sort of place, this alley, with drab houses half falling to bits and a general air of neglect. One of the houses was empty and I stood staring at it for a bit, thinking hard. I was remembering that I knew the owner, and after a moment I set off to see her.

Mrs Orr was standing at the counter of her shop, a general store at the corner of the alley. She was leaning her elbows on the counter, and I daresay she was glad of a rest for she was a big woman, all of sixteen stone at a guess. On one side of the dark wooden counter stood the big brass scales for weighing sweets and peas and barley, lentils and sugar ... Mrs Orr had a vast range of goods in her tiny shop. There was bacon and bread, milk and medicines, socks and shirts, ling fish hanging by the door and salt herrings in a barrel, molasses and tea and scented snuff – yes, and you could even get your coal there too. That shop was our supermarket long before the word was thought of.

When I entered she looked up, startled at the strange old tramp I now appeared, although I was only twenty.

'Good morning, Mrs Orr. Do you own that empty house down the alley?'

She asked, 'Who are you?' and I said, 'Look at me . . . '

'You're Willie Mullan.' There was pity in her tone.

'That's right, I am.'

She did not turn away as the others had done. A look of sympathy crossed her face. 'Do you want the house then Willie?' she asked.

'I'd like to live in it if you'll let me have it,' I said.

She put up a hand to the wall behind her, making the long fly paper with its dozens of dead victims stir in the air current, and took a key from a hook.

'There you are son, it's yours.'

I took the key and tried to thank her. Then I went to inspect 'my' house, and it seemed her kindness warmed me all the way.

To be sure the place was nothing to boast about. A poor, derelict old house it was, with the slates off the roof in a dozen places and half the floor tiles broken. Still it was to be my home and I looked over it with a feeling of satisfaction. There was a living room, about twelve feet square, with an open fireplace holding a crook for hanging pots on. A small bedroom filled the rest of the downstairs space and a loft, its floorboards rotting badly, stretched across the two lower rooms. No furniture, of course, but I was not bothered about a detail like that. I had a place of my own! That was something to be celebrated as soon as the pubs opened.

I don't think I had any intention at first of sharing my house with anyone. But when I got to the pub I talked with first one and then another, and a few of the bad lads began to realise that here was a place they could use for a card game or two . . . and in a very short time the house had become a gambling den for about a dozen men. I joined them at the card-playing; we soon got a big old table to play on, and then it was gambling every day and boozing every night, with pontoon the game and a 'pool' of sometimes over a hundred pounds.

You may wonder where a gang of down and outs would find that sort of money, but I can tell you they just put their heads together and planned a few crimes and it was as easy as winking to them.

I was not above a bit of trickery myself by then. One evening I won all the money in the pool by a little crafty trickery carried out with the aid of an accomplice. I considered it a neat piece of work and was pretty pleased with myself as I scooped up my money and made for the rickety stairway; I had an old overcoat in the loft where I meant to stow it away.

A footstep sounded behind me on the wooden treads and I spun round. It was a very bad fellow who had spent some years in prison; I saw he had a gun in his hand.

'You cheated,' he snarled. 'Half belongs to me or this is an accident.' And he levelled the gun at my ribs.

'O.K. Anything you say.' I made as though to put my right hand in my hip pocket, but my left hand went out like a piston and caught him full between the eyes. The gun went off and a bullet whistled past me to disappear through a hole in the slates. My accuser fell backwards and some of the gang dealt pretty roughly with him before throwing him out. As for me, I brushed off my hands and went to see what was cooking in the black pot over the fire; I was a tough character myself by this time.

Our cooking arrangements were of a rough and ready sort. A handful of sausages and a pan of potatoes, tea always on the brew, plenty of beer and tony wine. Sometimes we had a special treat when one of the lads would go out and steal a young lamb from one of the farms to roast for supper. One man actually stole a goat and killed it, but when he tried to skin it the smell was so appalling he had to bury it at night in a handy field.

We could usually find bits of wood to make a fire, and if we ran short there were all those rotting floorboards in the loft; we would tear up a few and burn them. Mind you, when it rained we would have showers from above coming right through the gaps in the roof and the spaces in the loft floor onto our heads below. We would have to shift round and put some old tin basins here and there to catch the water, but we weren't worried about a little thing like that, no not at all.

Of course we were all heavy drinkers to a man. We had an old bed that someone had found and an old lumpy mattress which we put in the bedroom, and if a fellow got too drunk and started making a nuisance of himself we used to throw him in there to sleep it off. Pretty often, though, we were all in the same state as the night wore on.

It goes without saying that the police became very interested in the old house down the alley. Indeed, it was soon considered the worst den of iniquity in the whole of Northern Ireland, as many police records bear witness. All sorts of horrible crimes and robberies were associated with the gang who were now my companions, and on occasion I joined them.

Once, I remember, we were raiding the house of a Canon of the church. He owned some good silver that we wanted to get our hands on. It was a rather daring business for we were attempting a daylight raid, knowing him to be out. Still, we felt as bold as brass that day, and even when I saw a police car turning into the drive it all seemed a bit of a joke.

'Looks like we've got company, boys!' I said. 'We'd better make for the back door.'

Well then it was everyone for himself and we scattered all ways. I went off down the street but I knew the police wouldn't be far behind once they had discovered the evidence of our raid. Looking around for cover I noticed a man on a ladder.

He was a bill-sticker, pasting a poster onto a roadside hoarding. Quick as a flash, I grabbed his spare brush and started slapping on the paste.

'Here, what's going on?' He leaned from his ladder. 'Who do you think you are? They never told me they were sending an assistant . . . '

'Well, you've got one now, mate!' I whistled and slapped as to the manner born as the police car cruised right by.

On one particular night one of the fellows went off saying

he'd bring back a few drinks. He did indeed; he broke into a pub and stole all the brandy he could lay hands on. Nothing cheap like old tony wine; my, that was a haul we really did appreciate.

We were playing cards that evening after the chap had set out. Hour after hour the pool money went back and forth as the cards were cut and dealt, cut and dealt again.

Sometime during the session someone must have ventured up the alley to the shabby old house, as a little piece of white paper was pushed under the door. I strolled over, picked it up, and read it carefully. It was a notice of a Mission in Newtownards Baptist Church with Dr Tocher from Templemore Hall, Belfast, as the preacher. I read it through and then turned to the boys.

'Nothing to concern us, lads. Just some sort of religious thing.' I screwed up the paper and threw it into the grate before taking up my game again. It lay there unheeded for the rest of the night.

It was around two o'clock in the morning when the fellow came back with his stolen drink. He burst in the door carrying a bag full of brandy, bottles and bottles of the stuff. No need to share – everyone had a bottle to himself, and very soon we were all lying around dead drunk with empty bottles in our hands. My, the police would have had no trouble catching that lot red-handed!

Now I got pretty drunk myself, but not as much as the others, and after a couple of hours I picked myself up and decided to get outside for a bit. The scene was a grim one; there were two men sprawled on the hearth, two more huddled on the stairs, another couple flat on their backs by the door, and all insensible with the drink. As for the smell, it was so bad that I reckon if anyone had struck a match to those brandy fumes we'd all have been blown to bits.

I stepped over them, got the door open, and then I was in the alley in the chill air of early morning; it must have been around half past four.

I felt low-spirited that morning, tired and fed-up with life. I walked along the alley, head down, and was just about to turn the corner when I nearly bumped into a chap who was going to work. He had come up the side of the footpath, and with me being still half drunk I had not heard him, but now I recognised him.

He was an odd sort of fellow to my way of thinking; he was always preaching in the streets; he would walk along a cinema queue with a Bible in his hand, giving the people a real lecture. We all thought he was mad.

Well, when I met this chap at that hour of the morning I thought I would give my spirits a lift by having a bit of fun with him, so I said, 'Hullo, it's a nice morning, isn't it? I see you're having a Mission at the Baptist church; I'm thinking of coming along some night.'

Of course I had no intention of going, but was just having a laugh at his expense, trying to make a fool of him. But that fellow wasn't as soft as I thought!

'Which night will you come?' His eyes were well open now and he was wide awake. He came closer and repeated his question.

I was taken aback and started to say, 'You know I'm drunk and was only fooling . . . ' Then something in his attitude seemed to strike me as a challenge.

'All right, I *will* come.'

He smiled. 'Right. You just fix the date and I'll come down for you and go with you.' So we made the date and he went his way. My, I had a queer sort of time then, wondering what I'd let myself in for, but I soon decided it would be a laugh and something to tell the boys afterwards when we had a drink or two inside us.

Sure enough the fellow did come for me and we walked along to the Mission, him in his best suit and me in my shabby old tramp's clothes, my toes sticking out of my shoes and my coat dirty and frayed. We went straight in at the door.

Because of the way I was dressed I quickly sat in the back seat. Anyway, I decided, from here I would be able to see all that went on and form my own opinion of the preacher.

I did form an opinion. I decided he was the biggest fool who ever lived.

In the first place, when I looked round the church, seemingly so grand to me, with all the pews polished and flowers

34

in the big brass vases and all the people crowding in till they took up every seat, why what was more natural than to expect some great figure of a man to stride up to the pulpit? Yet when Dr Tocher came from the vestry he was a poor old man of seventy or more and so lame on his feet that he had to be helped up the pulpit stairs. So that made me feel a bit sceptical.

I couldn't deny he gave out the first hymn in a good, clear voice. He had nothing wrong with his vocal chords, at anyrate; he had a fine singing voice, too, and his Scottish accent could be heard above all the rest. But when he began to preach his sermon I smiled to myself with scorn. The man was crazy, I was sure.

The thing was, he was preaching on a text from the Book of Revelation. 'And the kings of the earth, and the great men, and the rich men, and the chief captains ... said to the mountains and rocks, fall on us and hide us from the face of him that sitteth on the throne, and from the wrath of the Lamb; for the day of his wrath is come, and who shall be able to stand?'

I listened to every word, and the more I heard the more I thought the old man was a real fool. For how could anyone possibly know what was going to happen in the future? How could anyone be as sure as he seemed to be of what the kings of the earth would do years hence, or the great men and rich men and all the rest?

I did not know it then, but Dr Tocher was one of the most famous preachers in the British Isles, with great gifts of oratory and eloquence and skill in presenting difficult subjects such as this. Indeed, the congregation were listening spellbound as he reasoned and persuaded and talked about this day of wrath to come. It seemed that I alone was scornful of his message; I looked around me and came to the conclusion that he was conning the whole lot of them by plying on their fears, and a great anger began to build up inside me.

My rage exploded as soon as I got outside after the last hymn.

'How did you like the meeting?' The question came eagerly from the fellow who had taken me; his face was all

35

ashine with the hope that I was now a changed man.

He was soon disillusioned. I didn't wait till we were out of earshot of the building and of all the other good folk; I just stood there and cursed and swore and used every oath I could think of about that preacher – yes and about this fellow too, for getting me to go with him.

Poor chap, he kept edging away, looking scared, until he had put a good distance between us, but I still kept shouting and swearing and rubbing it in that I'd wasted my evening listening to a fool of a preacher who talked a lot of rubbish.

I certainly intended to make it clear that I didn't want to be invited again! I needn't have worried on that score, though, for I heard later that my companion had told a friend, 'I'll never take *him* to another meeting, it just makes him ten times worse.'

Well, I got some drink and went back to the gang. I knew now that all these people who called themselves Christians were fools and their preachers worse ones. I kept telling myself so, just to keep myself sure on the point. Day of wrath indeed! What concern was that to Willie Mullan?

A few nights later one of the boys came through the door just gasping with excitement.

'Boys, boys, I know where we can get five hundred quid in a day or two, and it'll be dead easy . . . '

My, everyone's ears pricked up at that! He turned to me and gave me a long stare.

'Willie, there's only one man of us who can make the plans to carry this thing through, and that's you. I know where the money is, but we shall need you to plot out the lie of the land and arrange the getaway. And there's no time to waste; you'd better start tomorrow morning.'

I was the youngest member of the gang, but I always did the organising on anything like this. That night I could scarcely sleep for thinking of all the wealth that was soon to be ours. I lay and made my plans; first I must survey all the land round about for four miles or so in each direction so we would know all the nearest exits in case of trouble; then I would need to have two or three taxis ready and waiting at the right time so that when the police got to hear of what had happened we would be well away.

I was out bright and early the next morning, and although I'd had my usual drink the previous evening I was fairly clear-headed, with all the excitement of the big job ahead to sober me up.

I worked my way all along one side of the site where the robbery was to take place and jumped down into a field in order to get a better view of the second side.

It was late October and the field was bare and brown. No seed would spring here until the following year. But another type of seed had been sown a short while ago and was already beginning to germinate. It was the seed which the 'fool of a preacher' had planted in my heart.

There was not a soul in sight as I began to walk along the boundary of that field. Just Willie Mullan and a late lark overhead – and suddenly a voice that spoke to me in my mind, direct and compelling. And the voice said, 'What about this day of wrath? What if you should meet God within the next step or two? What then?'

I stood absolutely still and spoke my thoughts aloud.

'But there *is* no day of wrath. As far as I can tell there is no God, no Heaven, no Hell, maybe there's *nothing* and we're just living for a little bit of time.'

I was getting myself worked up to carry on like that for a while, convincing myself I suppose, but the voice came again, insistent in my mind, 'But what if you should meet God within the next few minutes? What then?'

My, that voice really pulled me up. All my arguments just petered out into nothingness and I stood there all alone, looking up into the sky.

Suddenly, then, I knew that God was near. You know, I'd often heard my old mother talk about Him as a living God, but it was not until that moment that I knew he was there, a real and living presence. It was as though he had stepped out from behind a cloud and said, 'Here I am', it was as vivid as that.

Well then I thought that if God was indeed there in that field with me he might righteously pack me off to the lowest caverns of the damned, for I knew he was a holy God and I was a boozer and a rebel and a bad lot who was planning a crime at that very moment, and what else could he do with a sinner such as me? I trembled with fear and found myself speaking in the tones of a criminal giving himself up. 'All right, all right, you're God and I'm a black sinner, so if you take me and damn me for ever I know it's all I deserve.' And I just stood there, waiting, and shaking worse than ever.

Then there came a soft voice in my conscience that said, 'What are you trembling about, Willie? Sure, God *loves* you!' And at that I felt all confused and didn't know what to think, for I had believed God only loved the people who went to church and sang hymns on Sundays; I never dreamed he would care anything at all for a poor, wretched creature like me. But the voice came again, louder and clearer this time, and it said, 'For God so loved the world . . . ' – and at that I said wonderingly, 'Well, it wouldn't be possible that he could love the whole great world and just leave out Willie Mullan.' So I came to the conclusion that the almighty creator of heaven and earth really did love and care about a thing – a shameful thing – like me.

It was as if a light was breaking in on me. All my mother's prayers, all of those Bible stories I had listened to at school, began to have meaning at last. I knew with certainty that God did love me, and that he had sent his son to die for me. For the first time I thought about the cross of Jesus and its meaning. Jesus, the Lamb of God, the sacrifice, meeting the requirements of a righteous God so that God might step out in grace and offer full, free, present and eternal salvation to all who would trust in Jesus. All that I had learned back in my childhood became real; the light of the Gospel was breaking in to my soul and I could see the truth of it for myself. God loved me! Jesus died for me! If I would only trust in him I would have eternal life.

I felt as though a thunderbolt had hit my soul. I just stood there in the field and took off my cap and screwed it into a rope, twisting it round and round in my hands. All I had to do was to give my life to the Lord and I would receive new power for living. I opened my mouth to find the words to say.

Ah, but the devil doesn't give up that easily. At that moment another thought came snaking into my head. 'What about your pals? Sure, if you go back to that house without getting these plans made for the robbery they'll kill you, as like as not. And what about the drink? You couldn't get past the first pub and you know it. You haven't a hope of breaking with your old life; you're too deep in it now.'

I felt I was pushed into a corner. I could see clearly that Jesus Christ would cleanse me and save me and start me on the way to Heaven whilst my pals and the booze would lead me to Hell, yet the hope of breaking with my old ways seemed so slim. Yet God was so near me, waiting. I had to do *something*. One way or the other I had to make my decision.

I took a deep breath. Then I mustered up just everything that was in me and I said, 'Lord Jesus, on this spot today I will give you my life and trust you as my personal Saviour' – and in that second I knew I was born again. There was no preacher present, no 'decision card', nobody to witness my words, but in an instant my life was transformed and all the joy and peace of the love of God came flooding into my heart. My mother's prayers were being answered now, and a new life for Willie Mullan had begun.

4: New life

I crawled through the hedge and stood looking up and down the road. I felt a tremendous urge to tell someone what had happened, and after a moment or two I spotted a fellow coming along, so I beckoned him.

'Come here a minute. Do you see that field there? Well, I met the Saviour there just two minutes ago.'

My words did not have the result I had hoped for. The poor chap gave me one startled look and went scurrying off across the road; he kept looking back over his shoulder in case I was coming after him. He must have thought I was from some lunatic asylum!

I started walking and soon I saw another man coming along. 'Say mister,' I called, 'do you see that field over there? Well, I met the Saviour there five minutes ago.'

This man did not run away. He was a good Christian (I learned later that his name was Henry Todd) and he looked at me with interest.

'Is this right son?' he asked.

All I could say was, 'I met him. I accepted him. I'm saved.' But I guess there was something about my face that convinced him I was telling the truth.

That dear man just put his hand over mine and big tears rolled down his cheeks. 'Son,' he said, 'don't be afraid of tomorrow or of any of the demands life makes of you now, because the one who saved you today will keep you for all eternity.' We walked up the road together, and when we came to the crossroads he patted me on the back and went his way. As for me, I turned my face towards the old house in the alley, for I knew I could never go on with the plans for the robbery after what had happened. I had to go back to the dozen or so men who were waiting at the house, and I knew all too well that if I went through the door and told them, 'Boys, I'm not going on with this; I'm finished with you,' in that second I might lose my life.

That is no exaggeration. Every one of those men carried a loaded revolver, and many times when we were playing cards a fellow who was losing heavily would get out his gun and put it on the table and just look at you – and believe me, it was enough to keep you from winning, sure enough! And to back out of a job as I was about to do was asking for trouble; it meant that I was a dangerous character to them, with information that must not be 'leaked'. They would reason I'd be better out of the way.

Well, I was no angel myself. I carried a razor in a pouch at my belt, and had practised taking it out so often that I could have it out and open in a split second. I knew that with an open razor in my hand I could hold off one or two, at least, and that would give me a little time. So as I stood there at the crossroads I whipped it out and said, 'Lord, I've got to face them. I'll go back and tell them I'm saved, and the first man that opens his mouth against you will get his head cut off.' Wasn't that a good start for a Christian?

But just as that moment the Lord taught me a big lesson, because as I stood there an aeroplane passed overhead. I knew whose it was; it was called 'Finian the White', and it was used by Lord Londonderry for teaching young pilots to fly. You see it was twin-controlled, and while the young pilot sat in the front seat an older pilot sat behind, and when the younger man got the plane out of control, why the other would just switch on to his own instruments and carry on the lesson.

And as this plane went overhead it seemed as though the Lord said to me, 'That's how it's done, Willie. You're not in control any more; let me take over.' And do you know, I was learning quickly; I just went over to a little river and dropped that razor right in.

'Well Lord,' I said, 'you'll just have to do it all now. I've nothing and no one but you. I've got to go and face these fellows, and only you know what will happen, but I'm trusting you.' I had owned him in that field as my Saviour; now I was making him my Master and Lord.

I walked on, thinking what I would say (I would have to say something and then leave the rest to him) – when round the corner as I got to the alley came one of the worst of the gang.

I don't mind admitting that my heart gave a great lurch. The chap's name was Paddy Hanna; he was a big, dark fellow, broad as a door and as strong as a lion. I can tell you, he could go for you like a tiger, and when he lifted you up you wouldn't remember anything that happened afterwards!

In an instant I tightened my grip, as it were, on the Lord, asking him to help me. Then I said, 'Paddy, I've got something serious to say to you.'

I saw him lumbering towards me and instinctively got my feet into the right position to move pretty quick if he came for me. Although I was a saved man now, I didn't intend to get thrown about.

I took a deep breath. 'Now look, Paddy, I met the Saviour today and I got saved, and I can't go with you any more.' It was said, and I waited for his rage to burst.

But nothing happened. To my amazement he hung his head and when he looked up there were tears in his eyes.

'God bless you son; I wish I could say the same.'

Now I *really* knew the Lord was on my side! Paddy went on, 'Do you want those fellows out of the house? Come on then; I'll turf them out for you.' I followed him down the alley feeling like a small boy. When he reached the door he threw it open with a crash.

'Lift those guns; lift that money; lift those cards and get out. This fellow's got religion; get out.' Those were his words, and there wasn't a man there who dared do anything but obey. They all got up slowly and walked past me through the door. I never looked up – I hadn't the courage – but just stood there, and when the last man had gone Paddy said, 'God bless you, son; I hope I get saved some day.' Then he too walked out of the house. I was alone.

After the last man had gone a great, silent peace seemed to

settle over the tumbledown old house. I crossed the room and shut the door, and an immense feeling of wonder, awe and gratitude began welling up inside me. For the first time in my life I had seen the power of God at work, altering circumstances where no change was humanly possible. I knew that only a miracle could have saved my life and turned away the anger of those vicious men; only a miracle could have made a champion for God out of a hard man like Paddy Hanna. Only a miracle could have changed the heart of a hard drinking, criminal layabout such as I had become. God – the almighty creator of the universe – had worked a whole series of miracles in the life of Willie Mullan. I just went down on the floor, prostrate before my God, overwhelmed by his love.

I don't know how many hours I spent there, lying on the broken tiles of that old stone floor. Time ceased to have any meaning as I poured out my heart to the Lord. Night came, and the grey light of early dawn, and still I prayed on and on.

'Lord, you've done everything for me. You've saved me from all that wicked past. You've *saved* me; I'm yours now. You've freed me; I belong to you from now on. Oh, how can I thank you for meeting me in that field? I've been a captain in the devil's army; oh, make me a general in yours! Lord, help me to do something with my life for you, to show you how I love you. Take me carefully; lead me in the right way and help me to do the right thing. I'm such a poor, weak creature, I'll just be needing you every step of the way. Take my hand . . .'

That was a night of prayer, a man alone with his God, and surely a host of wondering angels hovering in holy joy. A den of robbers, an evil shack of a place, had become the ground where Heaven and earth met that night, and the mystery of the love of God for man became a reality within my heart.

When the dawn of Friday morning lit up the room I got up and looked about me. Then I walked across to the half bottle of tony wine that was standing on the table and tipped it down the sink. I could have laughed, I felt so exultant and free, as free as a boy. I set to then and made myself some tea and sliced some bread, and for the first time in many years bowed my head and thanked God for my simple breakfast and asked him to direct me through the day. Like Paul on the Damascus road, my prayer was, 'Lord, what wilt thou have me do?' I ate my meal with real enjoyment, confident that he would give me the answer.

Well, the first thing was to look for work. Up to now I had never paid a penny rent for the house; now that must be remedied and I must begin to take my place among my fellows as a responsible member of the community. At half past eight I said a quick prayer for help and then walked round to the nursery of the famous rose growers, Alexander Dickson and Son.

I waited on the path near the office. I knew the boss, 'Master George', by sight, and sure enough he soon arrived, looking immaculate in white trousers and shirt and smart hat. The contrast to my appearance could not have been more marked.

'Excuse me, Sir,' I removed my shabby cap.

'Yes?' The word was barked out. He looked me up and down.

'Sir, I am looking for work,' I got out.

He looked sceptical. 'You? You've not worked for years.' He only needed one glance to tell him that.

'No sir, but I decided yesterday to live a new life. Please give me a chance.' Inwardly I was praying, 'Lord, help him to help me.' He gave me one keen stare.

'Start Monday. See the foreman.' He was gone. I had got a job! I went back home, praying my thankfulness all the way.

That was Friday. Saturday, I knew, posed another problem. I had a bit of money in my pocket, and all the pubs in the town would be waiting to welcome me, like the devil's advocates, one posted on every corner.

Well, I had to buy food, so off I went through the town on a morning of pouring rain. My shoes leaked – in fact they were practically soleless – and the skies were grey, but I just looked up into those rainswept skies and smiled and sang, I was so happy. I talked to my Lord like a friend, and there wasn't a pub in Ireland could have got me inside that day.

There wasn't any question as to what I should do on Sunday. I was a Christian now, and Christian people went to church, didn't they? Sure, then, and I would join my praise with theirs. The only problem was, which church should I choose?

Something told me it was not going to be too easy. Many of the townspeople knew me as the black sheep of my family, and many had openly said I was past redemption, a thoroughly bad lot. Some, perhaps, had more righteous talk than Christian charity; some made dressing up in their best clothes a top priority – like the ones outside the first church I came to on that Sunday morning.

Well, there was nothing wrong in them looking nice. Did I imagine a certain smugness as I watched them shaking hands with each other on their way into church? Certainly I felt utterly left out in my ragged coat done up with a safety pin and my frayed shirt and worn-out shoes. I walked on, looking for another church.

The next one I came to was a big, imposing place, and I felt sure I would never feel at home there. Just then, though, I remembered the plain little Baptist church where I had heard Dr Tocher preach.

When I got there I couldn't pluck up the courage to go in. I stood over the road and watched the people arrive and take a hymn book from the man at the door. And do you know, that good man looked out and saw me, and came right across the road to me, a tramp in old clothes, and said, 'Do you want to come in? You're welcome.' He found me a seat and a young girl came and sat next to me and found the places in her Bible to share with me for the reading. That young girl is now a missionary, Mrs Dorrie Gunning, with over thirty years' service in South America, but I can tell you she was already a missionary that day to a new Christian called Willie Mullan.

All the way home I was thinking of the text the preacher had read, 'He shall not fail,' from Isaiah 42. And I talked about it to myself as I walked. 'He shall not fail *you*' – that means tomorrow at the new job. 'He shall not fail you' – that means in the drink problem . . . I knew it was true, and could hardly wait to get back to the church for the evening service.

That night I was given a present – and that didn't happen every day to a chap like me! Yes, they gave me a Bible at the Baptist church, and before I slept that night I read Ephesians chapter 6.

'Servants, be obedient to your masters, as unto Christ, not with eye-service as men pleasers, but as the servants of Christ, doing the will of God from the heart.'

So that was how God wanted me to work under Mr George Dickson. I decided to make a good start by being on time at seven next morning; in fact I got there at six-forty-five.

My first job was to wash flowerpots in a big tub of icy cold water. My, there's a job to daunt the spirits of a man on a chilly morning! The rest of the workers thought I was a great fool, getting down to the job at seven; they would lounge around talking or even playing cards until the time the boss was expected to arrive. One day he *did* appear, well before his usual time, and he looked in disgust at them all, scuttling off to find some work. Then he turned to me, up to the elbows in my tub.

'It seems you are the only honest man I have.'

I replied, 'Well sir, I don't really work for you; I work for Jesus Christ.'

He gave me an astonished look and walked away. I could tell he was thinking he'd got some sort of religious maniac here right enough. I smiled to myself. After all, I had been a fool for the devil all these years. Now I would be a fool for Christ, and count it a privilege, indeed.

I had got myself smartened up a bit by now, and I soon got promoted from washing the flowerpots. During the years which followed I grew to know and love the roses for which Dicksons had become renowned. Just by looking at them I could name up to seven hundred. Beautiful, fragrant Ophelia, softly pink; Betty Uprichard, vigorous and salmon coloured; the brilliant blaze of cerise and salmon and orange that was lovely Shot Silk . . . After that there came a spell of work in the alpine section, where I learned to propagate helianthemum and saxifrage, dryas and dianthus, gentian-blue lithospermum and many, many others. Eventually, when a new manager took over roses, alpines and fruits, he made me his right-hand man, and in the responsible position which I then held I was to meet many of the firm's customers, some of them titled people.

5: Jigsaw – the pattern emerges

Have you ever been to Chelsea Flower Show and seen the grand arrangements of roses and the lovely alpine gardens with their mighty rock-formations all so naturally set deep in the soil? Or gone to Harrogate, perhaps, or seen the Empire Exhibition that was held at Glasgow? Well then, you may have seen some of the work of young Willie Mullan, for in those days I travelled the country with my boss, Mr Bunce, and many were the gold medals we brought back for Dicksons. It was fascinating work and I revelled in it, loving the beautiful plants among which my days were spent and enjoying talking with the interesting people I met.

I felt just full of health and vigour now, and this was the Lord's doing, for I was pushing myself to the limits both physically and mentally, yet I never felt overtired. Each night, after a long day's work at the nursery, I would go back to my little house in the alley and there, after my meal, I would take out my Bible and study until three or four in the morning. By now I had acquired some other books, like those of Dr Ironside, and with their help I began to deepen my knowledge of theology. But it was the Bible itself which enthralled me, enlightened me, gave me inspiration and spoke to me of the love of God in the lives of hundreds of his saints. I read and re-read the stories of Abraham and Moses, of Daniel and Ezekiel, of the kings and priests and prophets, and followed the journeyings over the years of the chosen people of God, that great nation, as they came gradually nearer to the longed-for event, the coming of the Messiah. And there, in my small, quiet room, with the rest of the world asleep, it seemed, I lingered over the Gospel stories of Jesus, feeding on his every word until I knew many passages of the Bible by heart. In those night-time vigils I just delighted to learn more and more of my Lord – and unbeknown to me, he was filling up the wells of scriptural knowledge in my mind for which I was able to draw during all the years of preaching which were to come.

I believe the Lord turned to good use even my past experiences, for it was surely those earlier nights of sleeping rough and waking cold and stiff in the early dawn which formed in me the habit of making do with a mere few hours of sleep. Even today I am awake and able to write or prepare my sermon notes in the very early, quiet hours while others sleep, and I am grateful to God for this extra bonus of time.

Now although I loved these quiet times dearly there were occasions when it was very hard to stick to my plan. After all, I was still a young chap; I was putting in a hard day's work, and like any other lad there were other interests which called for my time and attention. One of these was watching motor racing, and this was an area which the Lord used as a testing ground one day.

It happened like this. There was a plan that several of the lads from the Baptist church would go together to watch the big Ulster Tourist Trophy Race, and I was eager to join them. We arranged to meet at a good vantage point, Taylor's lamp, on one of the bends in the circuit. It was a specially good place, so good we knew we'd have to be up really early, even to the extent of getting there by four a.m.

Well, I had the day off work, and I was up, dressed and shaved by three! Talk about excited; there was no holding me!

And then I heard a quiet voice in my mind, and it said, 'Willie, would you not be better off with your Bible?'

Oh, how the battle raged within me then! 'Lord, you can't mean it,' I reasoned. 'Why, you know how much I've been looking forward to this day. You know I've been faithful in the time I've given to you; surely you wouldn't demand this special day as well? And the lads will be waiting . . . '

Somehow, though, I knew there was some particular reason why he did not want me at that race meeting. After another moment's struggle I just said, 'All right, Lord' – and

I climbed the stairs and settled down with my Bible and concordance.

Through the hours that followed I could hear at intervals the distant scream of tyres; the cheers of the crowds . . . and then, at three in the afternoon, I heard a terrible bang.

At once I knew what had happened. I ran out of the house and sped three hundred yards to the course and another hundred yards or so to Taylor's lamp, where I came to a horrified stop.

The scene was one of carnage. A car had spun off the track and seven people lay dead or dying among the panic-stricken onlookers. Right by Taylor's lamp I saw the appalling sight of a man's severed head. Stunned and sickened, I looked around for my friends, the lads I had meant to meet here.

It was not until later that I learned they had given up hope of meeting me after a bit and all moved off to another spot. We were all safe. I went back home very thoughtfully indeed, feeling that truly the Lord's hand was upon me. And if indeed this was for some special purpose, then it would demand my obedience – and this I was determined to give, unquestioningly from now on.

Something else happened during these years at the nursery which was to enrich my whole life. You know, you can set a young fellow to work practically all the daylight hours, and you can fill his nights with study, but he will still find the time to fall in love, and that is what I did! I found the girl who was to become the perfect wife for me, and my dear Mary and I were married and set to work to make the little house more of of a real home.

How poor we were – and how happy! I was earning a pathetically small salary by today's standards, and Mary was earning just fourteen shillings a week at Newtownard's spinning mill, but housekeeping was an adventure, and we felt as rich as lords in our love.

I remember I used to get home for a mid-day lunch-break and Mary would insist on being there too. She had a two-mile journey and I can see her now, running along the road, all dusty from the mill, her face alight with love, to come panting and laughing into my waiting arms . . . and I knew that my lonely days were over, and my heart swelled full with joy.

Nothing in my new life in any way changed my eagerness to serve the Lord. I still spent as long in study, working in a little upstairs room while Mary busied herself with her household tasks, and she encouraged me in every way in this.

Later we were to get another, better house, but I look back on those days with great affection. We owned very little, but Mary made light of even the problem of finding furniture.

'There's a bedroom suite in the stores window that would suit us fine,' she said one day. 'It's twenty pounds, but if we can manage two-and-sixpence a week . . .'

'Twenty pounds! You're mad, sure enough!' But I knew Mary by now. She was a grand manager of money – and do you know, we still have that suite today, a reminder of her careful housekeeping, and my pride in my young wife.

But no marriage can be happy and carefree all the time and there came a very anxious period for us both. Mary fell ill. She had lost her robust, healthy look and was getting increasingly breathless. I looked at her weak and wan appearance with some concern.

'Mary dear, it's the doctor we shall have to be getting,' I said one day.

Reluctantly she agreed and I sent for Dr Sam Park, our doctor, who was also the chief physician at the local hospital. He arranged for various tests to be made and when he had received the results he sent for me. He was looking unusually straight as I entered his surgery.

'Sit down, Willie. I'm sorry to say that the news is very grave. Mrs Mullan is going to die.'

'One day, yes,' I replied defensively, not willing to accept that it could possibly be in the foreseeable future.

'Listen! Mrs Mullan has pernicious anaemia. She cannot live longer than two years.'

Only two years! My mind was stunned by the ghastly thought. It was unthinkable, unbearable, impossible. Soon my natural resilience and my faith began to re-assert themselves. I felt led to seek a second medical opinion.

This doctor seemed slightly more hopeful. 'We'll try these

tablets first and follow them with a long course of injections and transfusions.'

Eighteen months later he was able to give me the glad news that the condition was under control. Thirty years later she is still in good health but Sam Park, who prophesied her early demise, is dead.

One day as I was working in the rose field a man walked across to stand beside me. I glanced up and said, 'Good morning, Sir.' I knew him well; he was Mr Alexander Calder, the famous surgeon and a brilliant man in his field.

Mr Calder had a large house and garden and I had helped him and his wife on several occasions to choose roses, finding them pleasant people and easy to talk to.

Now he stood watching me for a moment. Then: 'Willie,' he said, 'I want you to come and work for me. Will you do it?'

I rested on my spade. 'Well sir, I will just have to ask the Lord about that,' I replied.

He nodded courteously. 'You do that, and let me know the answer.'

As he walked away I was already lifting the matter to God in prayer, and soon I knew that I was to 'go forward'. I had a new job, one that was to prove helpful to me in many ways.

Whilst all this was going on there had been developments in my association with the Newtownards Baptist Church. A few weeks after that first Sunday when I was welcomed among them, I was baptised and accepted as a member. For some time I enjoyed the services and gained much help from the Bible study meetings and prayer meetings. I made many good friends, so when trouble came I took it hard.

The thing was, there was a division of opinion among the deacons and the church split into two factions, good Christian men in both, but seeing things from a differing standpoint. It was decided that one group should leave the church and start another meeting, rather than cause further trouble. Now I was just a newcomer and felt quite bewildered; what was I to do, stay or leave the church?

For a while I was very shaken at seeing men I respected in heated argument. What is this, at all? If this is how Christians behave, sure I might as well go back on the booze, I told myself.

Fortunately I had a good friend among the elders, a man named John Cousins, and he took me on one side.

'Willie, we aren't going to bother you with all the details of this disagreement. If you stay in the old church we will love you and remain your friends; if you want to come with those of us who are leaving, we shall welcome you in our fellowship.'

Ah, that was a sad and sorry time to be sure. I had to learn that even those who love the Lord can fail to agree, and I spent much time in prayer asking him to show me what to do.

Eventually I felt I should join the small company who were leaving the old church, and the following Sunday found me with about thirty or forty others in our new meeting-place, the Templar Hall, Newtownards. Mr Cousins was acting as minister and Mr Hugh Ledgerwood – a man who later helped me greatly by his illuminating conversations on Christian matters – was also giving pastoral service.

One Sunday I had a shock!

'Willie,' said Mr Cousins before the service, 'it's about time you said a few words from the pulpit. Why not make a start next Sunday?'

'Me?' I was astonished – and scared! 'Oh no, Mr Cousins, that's not for me, I'm sure.'

'Look, lad, you read your Bible don't you? Well, just promise me one thing. If the Lord says anything at all that helps you this week you'll stand up and tell us next Sunday morning, even if it only takes a few minutes. I'll see to all the rest of the service; is that a promise, now?'

Well, what could I say? That week when I was reading in Psalms I suddenly saw that in Psalm 37 there were steps for saints, like this: Trust in the Lord, Delight thyself in the Lord, Commit thy way unto the Lord, Rest in the Lord, Wait on the Lord.

So I took those words and described the 'steps' which I saw to the people on Sunday morning – and a miracle happened. I was completely unconscious that God was using my lips to move the hearts of the people. I had been a tramp, a gambler

53

and a drunkard, and all I could do was to talk in an almost childlike way of the love of God as I had come to know it, but as I gave that brief message from the Bible on that morning, the Lord made Willie Mullan a preacher. My hand was to the plough of preaching and I have never looked back.

As I left the assembly after that service Mr Cousins took my hand.

'Willie, the Lord is going to use you, my boy. We will do this again, and I will help you so that you can soon conduct the whole service.'

Soon I was taking meetings on my own, and after a bit invitations came for me to preach in other churches. I never wrote out a sermon; I just used to sit quietly with my Bible in the evenings while Mary sat sewing, or working about the house, and the Word of God would come alive in my heart and the Holy Spirit would form the thoughts which I would take to the people. And although people soon began asking me to come and tell of my conversion and bring a Gospel message in huts and little halls all over the place on almost every night of the week, I still knew the vital importance of keeping time for my own prayer and study, and still maintained those night-watches with my Lord.

Sometimes I had a revelation, like the time I read the phrase, 'The devil himself hath bonded the minds of them that believe not . . . lest the light of the glorious Gospel should shine in.' So the devil was afraid of the Gospel, was he? Then the preaching of the Gospel – the cross of Christ – was the ammunition to use against him. I had thrown away my razor-weapon; now I had a gun, the big gun of the Gospel!

'Oh, make me able to use my words well, fill me with your Holy Spirit, teach me more and more of this "cross-work"; use me . . . I'm only your messenger-boy, but do the work of an evangelist through me . . . '

Way off in the future was God's plan, hidden from my eyes. Truly the gifts of evangelism and teaching were to be mine through the Spirit. One day I would teach the biggest Bible Class in our land and continue long enough to see ministers from it set in many churches and missionaries going to all parts of the world, and men, women and children giving their lives to the Lord over many years, and none of it my doing, but only his . . .

The hidden future . . . Right now, though, there was another meeting to serve, at a little Gospel hall in the back of nowhere. I got on to my old bicycle and pedalled off in the familiar Irish rain, as happy as a sandboy.

About this time I found a friend called Sam McClean, a big six-footer, one of the best tenors in the land at that time. 'Mac' teamed up with me as a soloist whenever I was preaching, and many evenings now would see the two of us on our bikes, pedalling along the lanes, happy and carefree whatever the weather.

Often it rained really hard. I remember one evening when that relentless, lashing downpour just soaked the pair of us through and through. We dismounted at the door of the little Gospel hall at our journey's end like a couple of seals from the sea, water cascading from our saturated clothes and squelching shoes. Mac shook himself like a dog, giving one of his booming, infectious laughs as he slapped my wet back with his big hand.

'Well Willie lad, the Bible says "He hath promised, when thou passest through the waters I will be with thee"!' The sympathetic official of the church who opened the door with concern at our state must have been surprised to find us so cheerful about it.

I never caught a cold because of the weather. All those nights sleeping rough when I was a tramp had toughened me, and the Lord had already blessed me with a strong body which a doctor only recently likened to a Rolls-Royce. But even more important, there was the utter joy of being on his service. Mac and I were indeed two of the happiest young fellows in the world, and we would gladly have cycled to the North Pole, if that were possible and if our invitations had stretched that far. As it was, the list of engagements grew and grew . . . It was wartime now, and one day I was approached by a Methodist minister, the Reverend Beresford Lyons, whose church was at Comber.

'I want you to come and conduct three weeks of evangelistic meetings at my church, Willie, with Mac to sing. It

55

would mean a meeting every single night, but you know we've all these soldier lads and lassies stationed here; it's a wonderful opportunity. Will you do it?'

I knew it wasn't going to be easy. I was working long hours at my job, often accompanying Mr and Mrs Calder to run their boat when they took friends on a fishing trip, helping with the meals when they entertained at home, and generally acting as their 'right-hand man' as well as being the gardener.

In addition I had to remember the needs of my own family. Yes, during the years with the nursery and with Mr Calder two sons were born to Mary and me. We named them Donald and Michael and loved them dearly; Mary's duties, though, now lay at home and my frequent absences must have made her's a lonely life at times. I talked over this new venture with her.

'Why Willie dear, you must do what the Lord wants, and I'll be only too happy for you.' Not for the first time, I gave thanks for the wonderful blessing of a good wife.

Out of those meetings came an unexpected bonus. Two young men of the church had splendid voices and soon Mac's tenor was joined by the rich baritone and the deep bass of Sam Scott and Tom Donaldson. The solos became trios.

That was how the famous Ards Trio came into being. Over the years those lads were to become known throughout the British Isles and overseas, and their music was of the very highest standard. Mac was a council clerk, Scotty a milkman and Tom a grocer. Remembering my background we billed ourselves as 'The Trio and the Tramp.'

Soon we no longer felt like four individuals but a perfect team, our hearts, minds and wills united by God into complete harmony. The meetings and campaigns and rallies went on, week after week and month after month, yet we never had a misunderstanding or a discordant word between us. We sang on our way to meetings; we sang on the way home, and one day, I know, we shall sing together in Heaven. Mac is already there; I conducted his funeral last year. I cannot fully express how much the three meant to me. I loved them, each one, dearly.

Like me, the lads had other ties which could have demanded all their time; in fact they each had a sweetheart whom they later married. But we all knew that this was a vital time, a time when God was using us in a very special way. All over our land people's hearts were being turned to him and souls were being saved; old differences were resolved and the knowledge gave us such joy as we had never known.

We no longer had to cycle; Mr Joseph Bowsen of the Baptist church now drove us in his car to our appointments, and we were grateful, for we were travelling most evenings now, and Sundays too.

One Sunday I *did* have a free evening ahead.

'Do you know what I'd really like to do?' I asked Mary as we sat at lunch. 'I'd love to go to Belfast and hear Pastor William Wilson preach. That man has a wonderful way with words, I've heard, great crowds every time . . . I'd need to get there early, but if I started pretty soon . . .'

'Why Willie, how on earth were you thinking of getting there, to leave so early?'

'I'll walk, of course!' For some reason my bike must have been out of action, and I certainly had no spare money for a long bus ride.

'But that's all of ten miles each way! Now there's a great goose you are for sure . . . just you wait a moment, now . . .'

Mary went to a special little jug and took out some money.

'There, you'll find there's enough for your bus fare. Go on, take it; sure, it's only a bit I was putting by for something or other; nothing important . . .'

And Mary kissed me and sent me on my way with that loving smile of hers, little knowing that this day, too, was to be a milestone in my life.

Pastor Wilson and I actually met at the gate of the church. He looked tired and ill; as we met he said, 'You're Willie Mullan.'

I was surprised. How had this great man come to know my humble name? But he beckoned me round to the vestry.

'Willie, God has sent you here tonight. I am ill; I can manage to take the meeting but it is you who will do the preaching.'

I was aghast. Me preach in this great place? 'Oh, I couldn't,

57

Mr Wilson; I came to hear *you!*'

'It's already settled in my mind,' he said. 'This is of God, Willie. You will preach tonight.'

So alone in that vestry I just prayed for the Holy Spirit to give me utterance, and that night God just lifted up my simple preaching so that many souls were saved, people falling on their knees in repentance and praise.

After that it was not just the small meetings, but large city churches and auditoriums which called for the Trio and me, and much blessing followed our efforts.

Our itinerary now began to read like a travel guide: Ballymena, Coleraine, Portstewart, Portrush . . . Derry, Dundonald, Broughshane, Carryduff . . . Rathcoole, Milltown, Castlereagh . . . and at last we went even further afield, to conduct a two-week mission at the great Tent Hall, Glasgow.

Mr Calder gave me time off for this. He had always been sympathetic to my preaching activities, knowing that when I was at work for him I gave of my very best service; indeed in some respects I was by now like one of the family, sharing their meals at times and helping the children tend their beloved pony in the intervals of caring for the garden.

An estimated 1,600 people gathered every night at that Glasgow mission, and we saw men and women in their hundreds coming to the Lord. We felt with the Psalmist, 'The Lord of Hosts is with us'.

After it was all over, I went home to Mary and the babies tired but happy, thankful with all my heart to have been so used by the Lord. Now, I supposed, it was back to the quieter times and the smaller places. It was autumn, and in Mr Calder's garden the beans hung in long rows. I started to pick them, then looked up as I heard a step on the path.

Two men were coming down the garden. I knew them both; one was Mr Frank Forbes, Secretary of the Baptist Union of Ireland, and the other Mr James Shields, one of the Union's past Presidents. I paused in my work and waited.

Mr Shields spoke first.

'We want you to leave your present employment and come to work full time as the Official Evangelist of the Baptist

Union of Ireland. We will not make you go to college and Bible school; we think the Lord has shaped you out in his own way, and we know you are his man. Will you come, Willie?' Frank Forbes echoed his words.

Leave the surgeon? Leave this family I admired and respected so well? Leave this garden where I knew every plant, every flower? Six years I had been with Mr Calder now. And what about the Ards Trio? With my mind in a turmoil, all I could say was, 'I will need time to talk to the Lord about this, please,' and the two men nodded their agreement.

Deep in thought, I left the beans and went out to the nearby mountainside where the children's pony was put to graze. I went there sometime every morning to see he was all right, and now I sat down on a rock to watch him for a moment as he placidly cropped the short turf.

Suddenly my head was in my hands and I was praying, 'Lord, what do you want me to do? Tell me and I'll obey . . . '

Like a flash the answer came. A phrase from Deuteronomy blazed in my mind, as clear as lightning; 'Ye have compassed this mountain long enough. Turn you northward.'

I took out the pocket Bible I always carried and looked up the passage. Then I looked northwards – towards the Baptist Union office in Belfast, and I knew that the God of earth and heaven had spoken to me, Willie Mullan, his humble disciple, and I just fell on my knees there by that mountain rock, lost in wonder, love and praise. For a short while there was silence, broken only by the pony's peaceful grazing. Then I got up. There was work to be done in the garden – and later on I must tell the surgeon what had happened. Tell the Trio, too – and Mary.

6: A sad farewell

Well now, I knew Mary would gladly accept my new decision to become a full-time evangelist for the Baptist Union of Ireland. The Ards Trio, too, although they were sad that our ways must now often be apart, were glad for me in my new calling. But when it came to telling the surgeon that I was leaving his employ, sure, that was one of the most difficult things I have ever had to do in my life. I broke the news when we had arrived back from a journey together, and do you know, that good man and I just sat there in the car and cried.

'Is it really so, Willie?' he asked me. 'After all these years... ah, how are we going to do without you indeed? You are like one of the family.'

I remembered the hundreds of little joys and sorrows I had shared with the Calders. Days of great happiness when in June Mrs Calder brought friends to admire the grand beds of roses I had planted on some cold November day previously. Days of anxiety when one of the children was ill, and of immense pride when Mr Calder received a Decoration from Her Majesty the Queen...

I thought back to the time when I had been first invited to share a meal with the family and their friends. Me, a poor Irish lad who had been a tramp, eating at a fine table set out with sparkling silver cutlery. Mrs Calder had noticed my nervousness at once and had given me a conspiratorial smile.

'Just you follow what I do, Willie, and you'll get along just fine.' So with each course, at her example, I picked up the right cutlery – and learned in that gracious, lovely setting lessons of social etiquette which were to stand me in good stead in the years to come.

Mr Calder moved a hand on the car wheel and brought me back to the present.

'If this is God's will for you, Willie, then I'll not stand in your way. Yes, I will certainly write you a testimonial.'

When I saw later what he had written, my heart was greatly moved. This is what he said:

Lotfass,
Newtownards, County Down.
29th Sept. 1947

Willie Mullan has asked me for a testimonial, and it is with very great pleasure that I testify to the high opinion I hold of his character and general ability. He entered my employment six years ago, and during these ensuing years I have had ample opportunity of assessing his character and ability. He has a very round knowledge of all types of horticulture and his keen eye for colour and artistic arrangement is far beyond that shown by the usual gardener.

His unassuming manner, kindly disposition, patent honesty and keen sense of loyalty make of him an employee in a thousand. One comes to look on him not so much as an employee but as a friend.

He leaves me to take up a new sphere of work, and mine is the loss. He carries with him my very best wishes for his future success, but above all his future happiness.

Alex M. Calder

A carefully arranged programme by the Baptist Union was to give me one week of rest for every three weeks preaching. It didn't work out that way, though! God poured out his blessings on so many meetings that I found myself taking missions at places all over the Province, practically non-stop. I became empowered with such spiritual and physical strength that a rest period was unnecessary, and in the 365 days of a year I preached 364 times. Indeed, I wonder what happened to me on that odd day!

Of course it all meant a lot of travel. As often as I could, I went home at night, but at one point, during a twenty-two week mission, all I could manage was a flying visit every Saturday to pick up a pile of clean shirts!

It was then that Mary came into her own special bit of ministry – I call it the ministry of the shirts! She developed the art of laundering and ironing them so perfectly that to this day I never wear a shirt that doesn't look brand new. Think of it, a clean shirt every day for over thirty years of marriage, and Mary still puts as much loving care into her ironing as in those early days. There are many ways of serving the Lord, and this is one of the gentle ways that many a young wife would do well to copy.

You know, when people are coming in great numbers, night after night, and turning to the Lord amid scenes of much praise, there will always be those who speak of revival and call the preacher a revivalist. For my part I have feared the word, and would never let it be used in connection with my labours for the Lord. I always say God blesses people in spite of me, not because of me. I am just a tramp who turned to him myself, and if I can lead others to him I am more than thankful.

I spent three years with the Baptist Union, and travelled many miles. At one period they provided me with a motor-caravan, a real little home on wheels, with a bunk bed, a table, cupboards for food and so on. At the back, when opened up, it had a mobile platform – I had no need to go looking around for a handy soap-box to conduct my missions! With this van I went to the Irish fairs and cattle sales where I could find men who would never be seen in a church, farmers and cattle dealers in the main. They were busy men, and this was no place for holding an hour-long service! 'Boys,' I would call, 'will you give me ten minutes now?' I knew they would gather round amiably enough for that brief while, if only out of curiosity, so I just put all I had into 'punching home' the message of God's love in a few sentences, and the Spirit helped me to reach many a heart. I learned, too, the discipline of keeping to my time limits, and so a spirit of good-will was established. In the evenings I would be at the nearest church to preach, and so the days went by.

Needless to say, I appreciated deeply the hours which I could spend at home with my family. Being away so much helped me to value those times all the more, and to thank God for this great blessing. Of course, one of the things I would have to do whenever I got back from a trip would be to go through the letters which had accumulated while I was away.

One sunny June morning in 1950 I was sitting at my desk penning an answer to a friend's letter when the postman brought the morning's mail. I picked up the top envelope and glanced at it before slitting it open.

Well, here was a surprise! On the sheet of paper inside the envelope was an invitation to become the Pastor of the Baptist church at Bloomfield, at the east end of Belfast.

A full-time pastorate! For the first time I contemplated what it would be like to leave the itinerant ministry which was now my life and to concentrate on being a shepherd of the sheep to just one church, taking spiritual responsibility for each of its members, counselling, guiding . . . I began to re-read the letter.

Its contents were quite straightforward. The deacons of the church offered a fair salary, subject to 'a suitable increase or decrease after one year according to Mr Mullan's ministry improving the church finances or otherwise.' No beating about the bush there! The letter went on to ask me to pray earnestly about the matter, and ended, 'whatever the Lord may allow we must gladly accept for his glory.' There was only one thing to do – I started praying about it at once, and very seriously, for I knew this would be a turning point in my life if I were to accept the invitation.

Soon, at God's clear leading, I *did* accept. I had been pondering the words 'this is the way', and I heard a voice saying 'Walk ye in it.' It was as certain and sure as that. So timidly, like Paul going to Corinth, I left my work with the Baptist Union, and with their blessing went to take up my new duties as Pastor of Bloomfield Baptist Church.

There was one thing about Bloomfield that would have lifted any heart. It was a newly erected building, and certainly one of the nicest in Belfast. As I stood before the congregation on my first Sunday I could look round on a beautiful new church, the sunlight streaming through the windows on to polished pews and lovely flower arrangements, and feel it was a place worthy of our worship. The membership was not large – about seventy people – but I saw a kindly welcome and a deep sincerity on many faces, and thanked God for guiding me thus far.

Mind you, knowing my congregation to be good, kindly folk was one thing; undertaking my new responsibilities on their behalf was another, and indeed I stood in the pulpit that day in fear and trembling. I had for years loved to preach the Gospel of Christ, but this would be something entirely new. Now I would have to 'feed the flock' week by week in this one place; now I would need to learn how to be a shepherd to my sheep, to comfort and console, to exhort and encourage . . . and above all to be an example myself to those I sought to lead in the Christian way.

Well, I must trust Christ and obey him, and by life and lip exalt him as much as was in my power. With great gladness I took up the challenge of my first pastorate and went to shake hands with as many of my folk as possible after the service.

On that first Sunday evening the church was filled to capacity. There was an atmosphere of hope, and as I preached the Good News of Jesus a man broke down and wept as he surrendered his life to the Lord. It seemed to me like a seal of God's favour on the step I had taken, and my heart was full of praise.

Soon the congregation was growing every week. The building was packed, chairs in the aisles, overflow rooms in the vestry, school rooms and church hall, and people talking about a revival coming to Belfast. But I wanted to cry out, 'No! No!' I had not brought a revival; all I had done was to obey my Lord, and he was sending the blessing. He was opening the window of heaven as he promised in his Word, and indeed there was barely room enough to receive it. One night the Prime Minister's private detective, John Carson, was saved, and now there came a flood of souls surrendered to the Lord; time would fail to name them all. In the Sunday services, at Bible classes and prayer meetings it went on, blessings given and great joy experienced; it was a wonderful time.

For Willie Mullan, though, it was not all plain sailing. Oh yes, I had the joy all right, but do you know, the more God made his presence felt at Bloomfield, the more I became afraid. For who was I, that I should be put at the head of an ever-growing flock like this? A lad from a poverty-stricken home who had been a drunkard and a tramp – who was I, indeed, to receive such favour? And to be able to bear the responsibility for all these souls entrusted to my care?

There was even a more subtle danger, that the praise I was getting and all the talk of revival might turn my head. I really did need to keep my feet firmly on the ground! More – I needed to keep my *knees* on the ground; the more the crowds grew, the more I had to find time to be alone with God.

Fortunately the church had several fine, understanding men among the elders and deacons. Men like James Fitzsimmons, Stewart Bossence, E.B.O'Reilly, Bob Winter and Joe Quinn. They realised I was still a young man and gave me much prayerful support.

Joe Quinn in particular was a grand friend. A dear old saintly soul of over eighty, he lived with his daughter Greta in a modest home where Joe spent hours of every day with his Bible – many said he knew it from cover to cover.

Joe understood my need for times of quiet. 'Look, lad,' he said one day, 'I'm giving you a key to my house. Here, take it; you're to use it whenever you want a bit of a talk or just a bit of peace and quiet away from the folk. Remember, you can use it at any time.'

Well, I did use that key, and one day it brought me a lovely experience. Like many folk of his age, Joe had grown a little deaf, and on this occasion he didn't hear as I turned the key in the lock. I stepped into the hall, closing the door behind me, and stood waiting for a few moments, hearing Joe's voice.

No, he did not have company, I soon realised. He was reading his Bible aloud. With my hand on the door knob, I paused to listen.

The words were familiar ones from John's Gospel, but there was something different about Joe's method of reading.

'Let not your heart be troubled, Joe.'

'You believe in God; believe also in me, Joe . . . '

I smiled, alone in the hall. Why, the dear old soul was reading as though God was in the room and actually speaking to him! As I opened the door and met the welcoming smile that lit the old man's face, I suddenly knew that God *was* in that room, his presence filled the place. And Joe Quinn was one of the men to whom I, a comparative beginner in the faith, had been sent to pastor! No wonder that my own Bible reading took on an even more fervent and personal note from that day on.

Not long after that Joe developed a serious illness and began suffering considerable pain in one of his legs. I spent most of three days and nights with him but neither prayer nor medicine took away his pain. At times he screamed in agony. I decided to call in a distinguished specialist. His face was grave as he delivered the verdict to me in a downstairs room.

'This is gangrene. His leg must be amputated. I'll leave you to tell him. I will come back for him this evening myself.'

Very slowly I climbed the stairs again. To say that I did not relish the task would be an understatement; I dreaded it.

'You are going to lose this leg, Joe,' I said as I settled myself uncomfortably at the end of the bed.

He shook his head. 'Oh no, I'm not, I'm taking this leg to the grave with me.' He paused as he considered another possibility. 'Or I'll be using it if the Lord comes first,' he said.

I had no wish to argue with him. 'We'll both pray and leave the outcome with the Lord. Remember, "All things work together for good," Joe,' I quoted, adding his own name to the text in the way that he himself was so fond of doing.

He smiled and laid his head back on the pillow.

When the specialist returned I at once told him that the intervening hours had been spent in prayer with Joe passionately believing that he could keep his leg.

'I am prepared to examine the leg again, to please him,' replied the surgeon, 'but I know we cannot save it.'

He repeated his examination of the morning, pausing to feel the pulse at the heel. A look of astonishment appeared on his face. He looked at me. 'Feel that,' he requested, 'blood is flowing.'

He turned to Joe. 'You old rascal, you have saved your leg.'

Joe's eyes were already closing as he began praying aloud his thanks to the Lord, and the specialist, too, bowed his head.

He still had two sound legs when he died ten years later, over ninety years old. At four a.m. one morning my telephone rang. It was Joe's daughter. 'Pastor, my daddy has just gone to heaven.'

'Greta,' I replied, 'he hadn't far to go, dear, for he lived on the border of that country all his life.'

7: David and some Jonathans

About this time someone came into my life who was to play a tremendous part in it, and who would become such a great friend that in twenty-five years we have never had a discordant word, though our views are far apart in many ways. It was as though God was sending me a brother – like David to Jonathan I can say of him, 'Thy love to me was wonderful,' and it still is. The man I refer to is Ian Paisley.

Dr Paisley is known throughout the world as Ireland's firebrand preacher – he is a very able politician and holds strong views which lead him to actions for which he has, in fact, gone to prison in times past. He is also, as Moderator of the Free Presbyterians in Ulster, a greatly gifted preacher, evangelist and teacher of the Scriptures. But there are many other sides to this great man's character, and some of them I have been privileged to know perhaps more than any other man. Let me tell you how we first met.

Often, before I preach at a special meeting, a prayer meeting is called, and when I can I like to join it. So on this occasion I was kneeling with just such a gathering at a place called Saintfield; someone was praying aloud when I became conscious of a man coming in and kneeling beside me. I moved up a bit to give him room and heard him say, 'Amen, Father', as the prayer ended. Then the newcomer himself began to pray.

My, what eloquence was there! What fervency! What utter sincerity – and my, what a mighty voice! Why, the man's words came out like thunder, great rolling phrases that seemed as if his very soul was being poured out in that place. As the meeting ended I got up from my knees and saw that the fellow had a figure to match the voice, with big shoulders and muscular arms, and a big, wide smile which he directed at me.

Ian Paisley had come to hear me preach. More, he had come with an invitation for me to come and preach at his church. He threw his big arm around me and said, 'Willie, you are welcome at our Tabernacle at any time. Will you come?'

I thanked him, and said, 'Ian, when I do come I will desire to know nothing among you save Christ and him crucified.' Right then I wanted to make it clear that politics was to have no part in my preaching, but he just gripped my shoulder more tightly and said, 'Willie, that is what we want you for.'

Not long afterwards I had the privilege of visiting his church for a three-week preaching campaign. Night after night the building was packed to the doors. On Sundays Ian hired the Ulster Hall which seated 2,200 people and again this was filled to capacity. A great hunger for the Word of God was strikingly evident and God visited his people in a mighty way.

You may think it strange that a man whose outlook was so different from mine should have wanted me to preach at his church. He was a Free Presbyterian, I a Separatist Baptist. His political views were not mine, a fact of which both of us could not help but be keenly aware. He passionately believed that the way forward for him was by immersing himself in politics. I, on the other hand, took no part in politics, believing that God had separated me to the preaching of a personal Gospel message.

But Ian Paisley is a complex character who has not been fully understood by the media or the public at large. He has suffered some terrible verbal attacks which were not, in my opinion, justified. His views on Roman Catholicism are well known for he has not attempted to conceal them. What is not so well known is his sincere concern for Catholics as individuals. I have seen him cry for Roman Catholics in their need and I have seen him give a pound note to a poverty-stricken Catholic woman.

The two of us have knelt alone in prayer month after month and my word, what times of prayer they were, times when heaven came near. When I lay ill in hospital Ian visited me every day, dropping down on his knees to pray out loud in a booming voice which must have been heard in the street outside. The boot was on the other foot when he was in prison. He always greeted me with a broad smile even in that time of adversity when the prison cell, instead of the hospital bed, was the place where prayer was wont to be made.

Once on a television interview I was questioned closely about my relationship with Ian Paisley, which certainly might give the impression of being an ill-assorted friendship. In particular, I was asked whether ministers of the Gospel should be in politics. For myself, the answer must be no but other ministers must decide for themselves; they are answerable to God and it is no place of mine to judge them.

One of the joys of Christianity is the rich fellowship which it brings. In the Old Testament David might be restricted to one bosom friend but Christians can expect to have many. If I have described my friendship with Ian Paisley as a David and Jonathan one, other people have used those words to describe my comradeship with Pastor H. H. Orr.

I first met Hugh Orr when he was pastor of the small Kilrea Baptist church in County Derry. I can see him now in my mind's eye as he was then. Tall and broad-shouldered, with jet black hair surmounting a handsome, finely-chiselled face. He was a countryman through and through with all a countryman's ways and an uncomplicated manner of thinking. He was big-hearted and lovable, totally incapable of any kind of deceit; the kind of man who if he brushed against evil it rolled away, an absolutely incompatible element.

He had a natural gift as a preacher and in my opinion he was one of the finest preachers in Ireland. All of us who knew him realised that the Lord would have greater work for him to do. He and I found ourselves co-speakers at a number of the conferences which take place annually in Northern Ireland. The partnership continued and developed when he accepted the call to be an evangelist with the Baptist Union and he and I together held many wonderful meetings throughout the province.

It is often said that the besetting sin of the Christian ministry is jealousy and I am afraid that it is sometimes true. But such a band of love existed between Hugh Orr and myself that jealousy was unthinkable. From a human standpoint we were at times competitors for the crowds that swarmed to our meetings, but we rejoiced at the blessings which came to each other's efforts. When God blessed me and hundreds of people were unable to get into the crowded building the delight in Hugh's smiling Irish eyes could be seen by everyone. I still consider him the greater preacher and when his meetings had wonderful results, love and joy just filled my heart. Cynics may laugh with scorn at our mutual admiration society. Well, let them. Earth holds no firmer virtue than Christian love.

When he received a call to the largest Baptist church in Ireland he was uncertain what to do and he asked my opinion. I believed the Lord was telling him to go forward and I told him so. It was my privilege to preach at his induction and a year later he and his church invited me to conduct a special three-week campaign at their premises in Great Victoria Street, Belfast.

'We're taking the Wellington Hall for the Sundays, though,' he told me. 'It seats about 2,000 with another 400 in the overflow room. I think we'll be needing it.'

We did indeed! Soon people were being turned away and one Sunday I arrived to find a dense crowd of about 400 trying to push their way to the doors; the place was already packed to capacity. I started to edge my way through the people.

Well, mostly they recognised me and managed to squeeze themselves tighter to make a way for me, but I had only got half-way when I met a real obstacle. It was a very large, very determined lady, doing her best to reach the door.

'Excuse me, Madam . . . ' My polite tap on her shoulder met with no response.

'Would you mind letting me through . . . ?'

She turned round then, and my, I thought she would eat me!

'What are you raving about, man? And who do you think you're shoving? Don't you know we *all* want to get in to hear Mr Mullan?'

I was then still a young man and I couldn't resist having a bit of fun at her expense. I tried to keep a straight face. 'But

71

Madam, I know the fellow, you see.'

She pulled herself up to her full height and glared at me. 'You? Do you think I can't see through that old trick? Just you get back into place; we've all come to hear this man and ...'

Someone in the crowd spoiled the fun. 'Dear, that's *him*!'

My, you should have seen that lady's face! It was all colours! I was laughing now, and after a moment of confusion she joined in shamefacedly.

'Look,' I suggested, 'just you link your arm in mine and we'll see what we can do.'

The rest of the crowd parted good-naturedly enough, and we marched in, arms linked, right up to the platform. There wasn't a seat anywhere else. Ah, but that night the dear soul surrendered her life to the Lord and was saved. Wasn't *that* something to gladden the heart, now?

Another lovely thing happened at Wellington Hall. One night there was the usual little group of people staying behind after the service for counselling and help, and after I had talked and prayed with most of them there was just one kneeling woman left.

I moved over to her and as I looked into her face I had a joyful surprise. It was my old infant school teacher, the woman who had made the Bible stories so real to young Willie Mullan years ago. Now it was my turn to deepen in her soul the knowledge and love of the Lord Jesus. And as we prayed together both our faces were wet with tears of joy.

Later in life Hugh Orr developed a heart condition and as he lay dying he asked his wife to arrange for me to preach the address at the graveside. Only one text seemed appropriate, 'For me to live is Christ and to die is gain.' Looking back over the years it was simply wonderful for a tramp like me to have a prince like him for a friend.

It was during the campaign at Great Victoria Street that a most unpleasant incident occurred which had remarkable consequences in the making of yet another lifelong friendship. It happened this way. When one of the evening meetings had just ended I noticed a young man waiting to speak to me. We went together into a side room and as soon as he sat down he began to cry in a very distressed manner. When he had controlled his emotions sufficiently he began to tell me his story. He was separated from his young wife but he very much wanted both to get his wife back and to put himself right with God.

'I want to begin life all over again,' he said. 'If there is a man in the country who she will listen to it is you because she thinks there is no one quite like you.'

'I am certainly prepared to go and see her tomorrow,' I replied, 'but first I shall need to know the whole truth. You didn't separate for nothing, now did you?'

He wept again. 'It was my fault,' he replied between his tears. 'I was running with another woman at night and I got V.D. My wife found out and the separation followed. But I am cured of the disease now and have a clean bill of health. Oh, I want so desperately to be able to put things right.'

I could not help but admire his openness and sincerity for I knew he was telling the truth. The next day I set myself up in the role of reconciler and sallied out to find the young woman who had been so shamefully treated. I found her in a very beautiful home and looking beautiful herself. As soon as she opened the door she recognised me, invited me in and began talking.

'Well, I suppose he was at the Mission last night and has been talking to you. Let me tell you, he never speaks the truth.'

'I think he told me the truth last night,' I replied and told her the sordid story.

'That's the first time he has admitted that to anyone. Now I shall be able to start divorce proceedings. I shall need you as a witness.'

To say that I was taken aback would be an understatement. I was momentarily floored. My efforts as a marriage counsellor were not turning out at all as I had hoped and planned.

At last I said, 'My dear, I came here as a reconciler. I don't believe in divorce. I can't go to court to help you obtain that and I won't go.'

I spent the next few days in some apprehension but when

several weeks passed by I concluded with some relief that she had thought better of it. Then out of the blue there came one morning a letter from a leading Queen's Counsel in Northern Ireland asking me to call at his chambers. He produced a typed statement setting out the young man's confession and requested me to sign it.

'Oh no,' I replied, 'I won't have anything to do with this,' and I got up and left the room.

A few days later I received a subpoena to appear at the High Court in Belfast. The net was closing in on me. I went to see the Chief Constable.

'Willie,' he said, 'you must appear and give witness. You have no option.'

'I will not do so, Sir,' I replied.

He looked very straight. 'Then you will be put in jail for one month for contempt of court or else fined a large sum of money.'

Next morning there arrived at my door a well-spoken gentleman. 'Good morning, Sir,' he said. 'I am Dr Crawford. Is it possible for me to have a talk with you?'

I had heard of him and his reputation. He was a superb doctor with a splendid practice. Later I was to learn that he was one of the greatest medical minds in the land and discover for myself that he was also one of the sweetest souls on earth. As he came indoors I was filled with curiosity as to the reason for his coming. He was a Presbyterian and I a Baptist and I could not imagine what he could possibly want with me.

'I hear great things of you,' he courteously remarked.

'And I hear great things of you, too,' I replied.

The civilities over he came quickly to the point. 'I learned yesterday about your subpoena,' he said. 'Do you really intend to stay silent in this matter?'

'Doctor, I was brought up rough and prison won't frighten me. I believe this divorce business is wrong and I won't be party to it no matter what happens to me.'

Then he told me that he had fought divorce and abortion all his life although he had difficulty in getting support for his views.

He rose and we shook hands. 'I am proud to know you –

let's be friends,' he said and continued, 'I came here this morning to tell you I am prepared to spend one thousand pounds to employ a good barrister and pay your fine.'

'No thank you, Doctor,' I hastily replied. 'I shall see it through on my own and I will not pay a fine no matter how long they imprison me. I will not surrender my principles. But I would greatly appreciate it if you will go with me to the High Court and stand beside me.'

So Henry, for that was his Christian name, drove me on the stipulated day to the High Court where we met Pastor Thompson who was then Secretary for the Baptist Union and who was also giving me moral support. As we mingled with the wigs and gowns a member of the legal profession who knew me came over and enquired, 'Willie, what are you doing here?'

I told him the bare outlines of the case. 'When my name is called,' I said, 'I am prepared to answer out of loyalty to the Queen; then I shall state my beliefs to the Judge and thereafter refuse to take part.'

'You will be in prison before tonight,' he replied. 'Please change your ideas.'

'No Sir, never!' I emphatically rejoined.

Pastor Thompson, Dr Crawford and I moved into the courtroom. Shortly afterwards the Lord Chief Justice entered at the other end and the whole court stood to attention. The doctor enquired in a whisper if I was still confident in what I was proposing to do and I nodded reassuringly.

Then it happened. To everyone's consternation the judge was suddenly taken ill and collapsed and had to be carried out before he could take his seat. The Clerk of the Court announced a ten-day adjournment and we were not slow in making ourselves scarce.

'Are you sure that you were not praying for something to happen to this judge?' asked Henry Crawford with a mock-serious face.

'Get thee behind me, Satan,' I retorted gleefully as the three of us walked briskly along the wide corridors of the building.

Before we reached the door at the end another barrister

came up to me and said, 'Follow me round to my office. It's not very far from the Court.'

We were surprised and puzzled but his tone sounded friendly, so wonderingly we obeyed. His room was stacked from floor to ceiling with massive tomes – law books by the thousand. He went along the shelves looking very intently, pulling out one book after another, turning the pages and shaking his head.

'There is something I need to find for you but I cannot remember the year,' he said.

It all sounded very mysterious to me for I had not the slightest idea what he was trying to do but it was no good my asking him for he had resumed his search. Suddenly his face lit up.

'Here it is,' he exclaimed. 'Willie, do you know my learned friend was wrong in subpoenaing you. There is a nineteenth century law which protects from court action a person who is honestly trying to reconcile husband and wife.'

He instructed his secretary to type out the details for me and we made a grateful farewell. It seemed that in ways beyond our understanding God was looking after me through the illness of a judge and the efforts of a kindly-disposed barrister who put himself out on my behalf. The news somehow reached the ears of the Q.C. who had sub-poenaed me and when the case was resumed a fortnight later I found to my relief and delight that I was not called.

For the next twenty years Henry Crawford called to see me almost every day. We went fishing together, bought new cars together and went on a pilgrimage to Palestine together. A friendship that crossed denominational barriers.

One morning in the early hours Mrs Crawford rang, saying, 'Come quickly, Henry has gone.'

I preached at his funeral when it seemed that almost the whole town turned out to pay their last respects to a great and good man. I sorely miss his daily visits although I cannot but rejoice that he is in another and better world.

8: The call to Lurgan

The loud ring of the front door bell jerked me out of my meditations. I closed the Bible and pushed the chair back. Probably one of the Bloomfield congregation with a problem, I thought as I made my way to the door. But there on the step were three strangers and I eyed them with some curiosity.

'We are elders from Lurgan Baptist Church and we would like to talk to you if we may,' their spokesman said.

Once inside and comfortably ensconced in my study they did not beat about the bush. 'We have been praying hard and we firmly believe that God would have you come to Lurgan.'

I stared hard at them. Were they joking? No, obviously not. Then they must be crazy. At Bloomfield I had a beautiful modern church, a large and increasing congregation, a successful ministry. Lurgan is a town in Armagh nearly thirty miles south-west of where we were sitting in the eastern part of Belfast. The church I knew was in a rather bad state and if I accepted this invitation it would involve a lowering of my income. It just did not make sense, but I did not want to be unkind so I promised to pray about it each day until I obtained clear guidance when I promised that I would let them know the result. They were quite satisfied with that and departed.

Long after that I was strangely disturbed and found it very difficult to settle to my work. I turned to my only source of help. 'Lord, you'll have to tell me about this. I'll meet you here every evening at five-thirty to see what you say.'

After some evenings with inconclusive results I heard an inner voice say quite distinctly, 'Read Acts 10.' I turned to the New Testament eager to see what message this chapter would hold for me. I rubbed my eyes with astonishment at the words which leapt from the printed page. 'Behold three men seek thee. Arise ... I have sent them.' Astonishment turned to fright. 'Lord, is that you, are you really talking to me?' For over an hour I remained on my knees, wrestling with my doubts and my reluctance to leave Bloomfield. But I knew I would have no peace until I surrendered to God's will and in the end I said, 'OK Lord, you win. I'll go to Lurgan.'

A strange peace was now in my heart and I wandered out into the kitchen to tell Mary. 'What do you think, dear, we're leaving here and going to Lurgan. The Lord has told me I must go and I trust him like I trust you.' Mary accepted the move quite philosophically as I knew she would.

The elders of Bloomfield were a rather different proposition and it was not at all easy for me to tell them. Stark unbelief registered in their faces. 'Man, you're mad. That would be to take completely the wrong turning.'

'It's not my choice at all. It's God's!' I gently reminded them. Eventually they had to accept that I believed with all my heart that this was God's will for me. So in the month of August, 1953, I came to Lurgan.

The deacons gave us a warm welcome; you might almost say they gave us the red carpet treatment for they bought us a new carpet studded with roses for the manse living room. The church there had been without a pastor for two years and it would have been reasonable to expect the work to be difficult, at least for the first few months. But the Lord had called me and I was assured that he would be my never-failing source of strength.

I can remember quite clearly the address which I gave the first Sunday morning. It was based on a verse in Philippians, 'The Lord is at hand.' The actual words I used, however, were taken from an old Quaker translation and have, I feel, a much more vivid impact – 'The Lord is at thine elbow.' As I expounded the Word I was very conscious of the nearness of the Lord. Some of the old members still talk about the reality of God's presence on that morning when glory filled our souls. In the evening of that memorable first day an old man gave his life to the Lord. Psychologists and church statistics alike tell us that conversions are a phenomenon of adolescence.

But this was a man who had long ago reached maturity and I felt it not only set the seal on my first day's ministry but was an earnest of even better things to come. So indeed it was to turn out.

One of the elders, John McGill, approached me that morning and said, 'Willie, it's our practice to hold the Bible Class in the little hall at the back of the church on Tuesdays. What do you intend doing?'

'John,' I replied, 'it will never be held there again. I propose announcing the Bible Class to be held in the church this coming Tuesday.'

He smiled dubiously. 'It's a big building for such a small class.'

I laughed. 'Let's trust God and see.'

The Lord was plainly at work. On that first Tuesday the church was half full and it never ceased to grow until standing room only was the order of the day. Some years later the church had to be extended to accommodate the people. The extension allowed for an additional 200 people but even this was not large enough and now 600 and sometimes as many as 800 crowd in to listen the God's Word. Some come from distant places and from other denominations; they are diverse in outlook and belief but they have at least one thing in common – an eagerness for the Word. But I am jumping ahead. Let's go back to the first few days in Lurgan.

When a family moves house the resultant uprooting is probably harder for the children than for any other members of the household. Young friendships are severed and there has to be the sometimes painful and difficult process of settling down into a new school. On the morning we arrived in Lurgan we were welcomed by our new next door neighbour who was the wife of the owner of a local supermarket.

'Your boys look nice lads,' she said. 'How old are they?'

'Michael, the youngest, is five and Donald is eleven,' I answered. 'Which reminds me,' I continued, 'I shall have to make arrangements for them to go to school. I suppose you wouldn't be able to tell me the best school in the town?'

'That I can,' she replied. 'It's King's Park without a doubt.'

That very afternoon I went to King's Park. The headmaster, however, shook his head as soon as he had learned the purpose of my visit. 'There is overcrowding in the classes now in both these age groups,' he said.

I pointed out that the boys' reports from the previous school were very creditable.

'Yes, I can see that,' he answered. 'But that doesn't manufacture any more space in my school, does it?'

I had to accept the logic of this and was just about to leave. He glanced again at the reports as he picked them up to return them to me. His eyes alighted on the name of the headmaster of their first school.

'Did you know this man at all?' he demanded.

'Yes, indeed, so I did,' I replied.

'What, then, do you think of him as a teacher?' he enquired.

'The best in the country,' I asserted. There was no point in false flattery by adding 'present company excepted'! He wasn't going to take the boys and that was that.

'I'm glad to hear you say that,' he said. 'I trained with him in college and I agree with your assessment of him. Bring your boys along next Monday!'

So that, too, was that.

My continuous heavy commitments in the work of the church prevented me from having as much time with them as I would have liked, but I was always glad to hear from their mother of the little adventures which made up the pattern of their days. As happens so often, the two bothers were quite different in temperament. Michael was a gentle, fastidious boy but Donny was tough and reckless. I remember that when he was a toddler a wealthy farmer friend bought a big toy car for him. In a couple of days he had carried out pretty successfully a wrecking assignment, pedalling his way with gusto into many items of furniture and even worse, smashing a little friend's bicycle.

As is often the case amongst brothers, Donny was not disposed to let his brotherly love be too much in evidence – at times rather the reverse! It took an accident for his real feelings to be displayed. Young Michael was racing at speed along the pavement and not looking where he was going he ran into a lamp-post. He reeled backwards and fell to the ground with blood pouring from a great gash in his head. Fortunately his elder brother was close at hand. Donny produced his handkerchief, bound up the wounds in best 'Good Samaritan' style and solicitously supported him home with great concern. When Michael had recovered we saw the funny side of Donny's action and for a while it was the standing family joke.

Donny was always an athletic type and when he reached his teens he developed an interest in judo. When Michael became a teenager he took up golf in a big way. I had mixed feelings about this. I was pleased that he was enjoying a healthy hobby and I bought him his first set of clubs with which he began to win cups and medals. But, on the other hand, I sensed that the game was becoming an obsession. More and more time was being spent on the course and I wondered whether he was going to get his priorities right. So, too, did his elder brother. When I paid Michael's entrance fee for the Boys' International Golf Tournament, which he promptly repaid by breaking the course record the day before the big event, Donny remonstrated with me.

'Do you know what you're doing Dad?' he expostulated. 'Mike's going to let golf take him away from the church.'

'Look, Donny, my son, you may be the first mate of the family ship but I'm the captain, so I am. I know what I'm doing all right. It would have been no good standing in his way for that would only have spurred him on. All the same for that, I don't particularly want him to win this Tournament tomorrow and I'm going to pray that he doesn't! You can do the same.'

Michael did not win and it was not until some time later that he learned his father and brother had been praying for him to lose! Neither of us need have worried about him. The captain of his club invited him to become a member of the adult team when he was only fifteen but he refused because the matches were played on Tuesdays, the Bible Class night. When he was sixteen he came home one day, threw his clubs into the corner and told us that he had given his life to Christ whilst on the course. From then on, golf ceased to have the same importance for him.

In the two churches in which I have been pastor there has always been a devoted Sunday school staff who have been concerned to bring the children into a living relationship with Jesus. My little grand-daughter Carolyn, when only five years old, bore her own simple, sweet, but eloquent testimony to the single-mindedness of her Sunday school teacher.

She looked up at my face towering above her and winsomely whispered with more than a dash of pride, 'Grandad, Robert only talks about Jesus.'

Many non-believers think that churches are full of elderly people and that religion is something you can put off thinking about until you are approaching your end. Well, there are plenty of elderly people in the Christian church it is true and thank God for that. If they have not gained wisdom by the time they have reached a ripe old age when will they achieve it? But if non-Christians genuinely think that it is only elderly people who go to church how mistaken can they get?

One Sunday after the evening meeting a young mother approached me. With her were her five-year-old twin daughters, two little charmers in identical blue dresses. She looked rather embarrassed.

'I don't like bothering you, Mr Mullan, but I don't quite know what to do. You see, they're so insistent,' she said.

'What's the trouble?' I enquired.

'Well, sure it's not exactly trouble,' she replied, 'but these little ones of mine say they want to be saved and I don't know how to answer them. I've told them that they are too young yet but they won't take no for an answer.'

'Come on in to the vestry and I'll have a chat with them,' I said.

If ever an interview needed delicate pastoral skill, this one did. They stood one on each side of me, crying softly as I held their hands. How tenderly I had to talk to them, but they wanted to give their little hearts to the Lord and they did. My youngest converts ever. Today they are mothers themselves and both remain committed Christians; one gave her

82

testimony recently at Lurgan and one is a Sunday school teacher.

Perhaps you think that this must be a record but you would be wrong. The wife of the Chief Constable of our town has a vivid memory of surrendering her life to the Saviour whilst holding on to her mother's apron at the tender age of four!

Yet interest in the life of the church is by no means restricted to children and elderly people but covers all age groups. One of the heartening signs in these difficult days is the large number of teenagers who are concerned about the meaning and purpose of life. In the church at Lurgan we have numbers of them meeting at the Friday night youth club. It is firmly Bible-based with the emphasis on Scripture quizzes and puzzles. They have rambles, picnics, weekends at the seaside and in the mountains but they do not have indoor games like table-tennis and billiards as in so many youth clubs. One year a special mission led by visiting youth workers was held when about 200 youngsters attended. Many of these progressed to active Christian witness.

Some time ago the church became concerned that this witness should develop in a more specific and concrete way and open-air meetings on a large scale were arranged in the summer months. Up to 300 young folk were transported in cars to the surrounding villages – quite a feat of organisation in itself. It was my job to plan the content of the meetings. They sang, gave convincing testimonies and a few of the more able gave short, seven-minute addresses. I used to give them mock threats if they exceeded the time limit. It is greatly to be regretted that in these times of trouble open-air meetings are not possible and this valuable work has had to come to an end.

A very different kind of youth work took place one year at Portadown College. It happened like this. The principal of the College, a good Christian man, phoned me at Lurgan to enquire if I would be willing to conduct a Teach-In. He said that about 100 students were shortly going on to University and he wanted a Christian minister to answer their many questions on the Christian faith.

'They are a highly critical bunch and they can question a

83

speaker relentlessly,' he warned.

'I'll have a go,' I said.

'That is good of you. To be honest, I naturally approached the local clergy first but they seemed alarmed at the prospect. Knowing the pupils as I do, I can't say that I blame them. Well, that's settled then. I can give you half an hour.'

'Half an hour! You must be joking. I shall need not less than two hours,' I stipulated.

'Oh, that's quite impossible. It would interfere with the curriculum,' he replied.

'The curriculum will have to be altered then if you want me to come. Those are my conditions,' I asserted.

'I shall have to consult with the staff,' he answered dubiously.

'You do that,' I said, 'and let me know the result.'

I got my two hours – and a very stimulating time it proved to be. Although I know that there are many Christians who could not accept my own particular doctrinal approach, I based my stand on a literal interpretation of the Scriptures. Before they began firing their questions I had a preliminary word.

'Let's get clear what this is all about. This is a battle for the Christian faith and let no mercy be given on either side.' I said. Something of my early pugnaciousness from my days as a tramp was beginning to re-assert itself.

The first questioner to rise to his feet was a tall, sixteen-year-old boy. 'Do you really believe that the sun, moon and stars were made on the fourth day of creation?' he asked.

'Indeed, I do,' I answered briefly, sensing that I had not heard the last of this particular question.

Sure enough, a 'supplementary' was on its way immediately. 'But how can that be?' he enquired. 'The sun must have been in existence before the vegetation.'

'Whoever told you that was talking a lot of blather,' I retorted. 'I used to work in a nursery so I know as well as you that plants need light. But what makes you think that the sun is the only source of light? When Paul was travelling down the Damascus road he saw a light *above* the brightness of the sun. When Peter was in prison it is stated that a light shone

84

in the cell. In the Book of Revelation we are told that in heaven there is no need of the sun. Clearly God has sources of light other than the sun.'

At the end of the session I received a standing ovation and later in an end of term essay many of the students said that the best day of the term for them was the day of the Teach-In.

I have always been a man to speak my mind and, at the risk of giving offence, if I thought someone was blathering I did not hesitate to say so. One evening I was addressing a convention at Newcastle in County Down. The chairman of the meeting was in great good humour and he decided to introduce me in a light-hearted way.

'Friends,' he said, 'our speaker tonight is a wild Irishman. The last time I saw him was a number of years ago when he was captain of a football team. They were playing a side from the local parish church in a cup match. And, would you believe it, this wild man perpetrated a blatant foul on the curate.'

I got up to begin my address. 'Friends,' I said, 'I know that you will realise that the unfortunate foul on the curate was a pure accident. But,' I added swiftly, 'if I had known then the rubbish which he preached from the pulpit I would have given him far more!'

9: The Word revolves around the world

One of the exciting developments of recent times is the way a church's ministry can be greatly extended by the modern miracle of recording. It was a joy to me when in 1957 Mr William Hewitt led a team of helpers in tape-recording the Tuesday Bible Class. Since then tapes have gone out across the world not only to the major cities like London, Berlin, New York and Los Angeles, but also to some extraordinarily remote places such as the jungles fringing the mighty Amazon, the dense equatorial rain forests of Africa and the barren deserts of Iraq.

It was in Iraq, at the site of the ancient biblical city of Ur of the Chaldees, that the tapes from Lurgan were heard in rather unusual circumstances – so I have been told. An oil company executive, who is responsible for a large oil well in the vicinity, played my messages to about forty intently listening Arabs squatting in typical fashion on the desert sand at midnight in the moonlight! So it was that the Christian Gospel made another small entry into the seemingly impenetrable world of Islam, and that rejoices my heart.

It is always exhilarating but strangely humbling when by the grace of God one's witness is spread across the world. I had a remarkable instance of that one morning. There was a knock on the door and there to my surprise stood a beautiful Maori girl from Timaroo, South Island, New Zealand. She had an amusing story to tell.

One Sunday morning at the Maori church which she attended there was a guest preacher from Belfast. In the course of his address he gave his personal testimony and said that he was saved through the preaching of a man from Lurgan called Willie Mullan.

He quickly added, 'I'm sure you've never heard of him.'

The whole congregation of about 400 erupted into loud laughter.

Puzzled, he turned to the pastor beside him on the rostrum and asked, 'Why are they laughing?'

The pastor rose to his feet. 'Will everyone here who has been converted through the words of William Mullan, please stand up.'

There was a rattle of chairs and shuffling of feet as about 200 Maoris, half the congregation, stood up. They had been listening to the Lurgan tapes for the last year and this was the result. It is to Christ and him alone that we must give the glory.

Have you ever pondered on the fact that God can make good come even out of our mistakes? A striking example of this occurred some time ago in connection with one of my tapes.

The scene is set in southern Argentina during the regime of the dictator General Juan Domingo Peron. It was a time of great unrest and parts of the country were in open revolt. Three missionaries, engaged in pioneering evangelical outreach, were taking the Gospel to the small towns in the sparsely inhabited southern region of Patagonia. Late one day they came to one such town and were dismayed to see displayed on the edge of the town a large notice proclaiming with brutal bluntness: 'Missionaries, keep out!' In view of the uncertainty of the political situation, with gangs of armed men roaming the streets of some cities, it seemed prudent to withdraw.

They set up camp for the night out on the barren plain and took counsel together. Due to the exceedingly low rainfall much of the area consisted of inhospitable scrub and even the most favourable parts were but dry savanna. Not a spot where it was easy for a traveller to live off the land, and they urgently needed access to the town in order to replenish their provisions. What were they to do? They were in a sore dilemma and although they talked at length they could not find an answer.

Now it so happened that they had ordered a consignment

of tapes consisting of a series of expositions on Romans which I had been delivering. A tape dealing with a chapter at a time was sent out to them as soon as the message was given. They had already received tapes on the first eight chapters and amongst their possessions was a small, unopened parcel supposedly containing the homily on chapter 9.

Suddenly one of them looked up and said, 'We've talked ourselves silly over this. We shan't make any more headway tonight. Let's relax and listen to the latest Willie Mullan tape. That is, if we can find it amongst all this paraphernalia. Sometimes I wish the funds would run to hotels – we'd need a lot less baggage and it would be more comfortable than a tent.'

'Quit moaning, brother. Remember the Lord had nowhere to lay his head and you've got a camp bed! Come and help me find the tape.'

'Let's see, it'll be Romans 8, won't it?' the third missionary enquired.

'No, we've already had that, it will be chapter 9. Ah, here it is.'

They squatted on the ground around the recorder. Then to their surprise and initial disappointment they heard my voice describing the Israelites approaching the Red Sea. Someone back in Lurgan had slipped up and despatched the wrong tape. This address was based on the words of the Lord, 'Speak unto the children of Israel that they go forward.' They listened in silence and when it ended the silence deepened. Each of them realised that God had spoken to them that night. Their problem had disappeared. The next day, their fears gone, their doubts evaporated, they walked boldly into the town distributing tracts and no one said them nay.

Revolutions, rebellions, guerilla warfare and terrorism seem the order of the day in these troublesome times and the missionary in my next story also had to live through a coup. The setting this time was not less barren steppes but a tropical island.

The situation of aliens in these conditions is often one of real danger. It certainly was for Ann, a lady worker alone at a missionary outpost. Shots could be heard in the distance, gradually getting nearer and nearer. Hastily gathering together a few belongings and a small supply of food, Ann escaped to the hills. The tropical heat was intense and myriads of flies buzzed around her as she struggled upwards on a barely discernible path through lush vegetation whose trailing, thorny stems scratched and scarred her. Reaching a small clearing she paused to look down at the lower ground. Puffs of smoke arose in the air and the acrid scent of gunfire reached her nostrils. This was no time to linger. Fear gave her added strength as she exerted all her efforts to get well away from the danger zone. Even so, the bundle she was carrying appeared to get heavier with every step. Mockingbirds, disturbed from the bushes, seemed to laugh at her plight.

At length, she came upon a half-ruined hut of corrugated iron and stumbled in exhausted. Shelter, of a kind, at last. Here she would have a little protection from the wild beasts, the poisonous snakes and the 'creepy-crawlies' of the jungle – a shield also from the tropical downpours, at least, so Ann thought. But when the torrential rain came during the night it beat upon the corrugated iron with a violence and a tempestuous din that was positively frightening.

Two days and nights went by. By the third day her meagre supply of food was dwindling. Despondently she looked out of the window. Then she remembered that amongst the few items of equipment she had brought was her precious tape-recorder. That's it, she thought, put on a tape to cheer myself up. Soon my Irish accent was filling the hut and sounding down the hillside.

Ann glanced out of the window again and, to her horror, saw on the slope below the figure of a soldier climbing up towards her. He was in combat uniform and carried a rifle. Her first panic-stricken reaction was to switch off the recorder. Then she realised that he had almost certainly heard the sound of my voice. In any case, he was bound to find her. She was doomed. Might as well leave it on and at least die with the companionship of another Christian voice.

A heavy boot kicked open the door. A shadow fell across the floor of the hut. Ann crouched in a corner, not daring to look up. The tape flowed on.

Then a voice broke in, 'That's Willie Mullan.'

Startled and amazed Ann looked up into the smiling face of an American soldier, a member of a force sent to relieve the island. God had sent another Christian to give succour to one of his children in need. Before he led her to safety the young soldier knelt on the earth floor to give thanks to him who had made the rescue possible.

The tapes still revolve around the world. As well as the Tuesday Bible Class the two sermons at the Sunday services are now recorded. We have over a thousand items in our catalogue. After expenses are met the profits go to the work of the Kingdom. Not just to our own church, you understand, but also to the mission field overseas, to people like Ann. Only a few weeks ago I was preaching in a small church in a small Ulster town. I took with me 250 tapes. Within ten minutes they were all sold. What joy to know the hunger for the Word.

A long time ago a little booklet was produced which gave an account of my conversion. It circulated widely in Ulster but has not travelled the world like the tapes. Nevertheless, one somehow found its way to a small Devonshire hamlet with a remarkable result. It was like this. A party of tourists was visiting the Benedictine Abbey of Buckfast. One of them, in fun, entered the confessional box and there he found the story of Willie Mullan. I do not know whether it surprised the holidaymaker but when I heard about it, it certainly astonished me. If in Palestine the Jews had no dealings with the Samaritans so in Northern Ireland Protestants and Roman Catholics do not have much to do with each other. What could my booklet be doing in the confessional? Perhaps a guilt-stricken Catholic had confessed to reading the booklet and it had been confiscated by a monk! Or perhaps the monk wanted to read it for himself! I shall probably never know. What I do know is that the tourist brought it out and later handed it to another member of the party who read it and in consequence was gloriously saved, praise the Lord!

10: Gathered fruit

The greatest joy that can come to any Christian must surely be that of pointing someone to the Saviour. When this happens to me, however, I am always filled with a mixture of conflicting emotions. There is, of course, elation. A soul who is precious in God's sight has turned from darkness into light. Who would not be excited? Then there is deep satisfaction. God's kingdom has been enlarged as yet another subject surrenders to his kingly rule. Christ's command to preach the Gospel has been effective. But amazement is present, too, for it all seems too wonderful to be true. And there is always humility; God is using an erstwhile tramp to play a tiny part in the fulfilment of his mighty purposes.

It has been a very humbling yet thrilling experience to point hundreds to the Lord. It is not my practice to make emotional appeals; I have found that God provides sufficient grace and power in the faithful proclamation of his Word to touch the hearts of the unconverted. Every conversion is different because every human is unique, but some, for various reasons, are more unusual than others. I want to share with you now just a handful of the highlights amongst the many conversions I have known.

In the Blue Hills of Donegal

Away in the far north-west of Ireland, in Donegal, is a hilly district known as the Bluestack mountains; they are ancient rocks which reach up to over 2,000 feet. Most of the local inhabitants are Roman Catholic, but I had been invited by a small group of Protestants to come and preach. The meeting place served to emphasise the rural nature of the area. It was a barn! A few of the Roman Catholics attended the meeting and all were kind and friendly to me.

One morning I strode out over the moors. A young man then, I enjoyed the brisk, bracing walk in the westerly breeze. Coming towards me was an old Irish lady of the kind who only seem to be found in the remote countryside. Her shining eyes indicated a vitality which belied her wrinkled, weather-beaten face. She wore a dark blouse, a woollen cardigan was draped over her shoulders and her long skirt reached down to the ground. On her back was a bundle of sticks for her fire.

'Good morning, mother. Can I carry your sticks?' I greeted her.

'That you can, my son,' she replied.

I picked up the bundle and turned round. We chatted inconsequentially about this and that although I took care to tell her who I was and what I was doing in her neighbourhood.

'That's good work, my son. May God bless you,' she said.

We came to her little thatched cottage with its characteristic 'stable' door that is so typical of the Ireland of yesteryear. I dropped the sticks, sat down on an old tree trunk and she sat down beside me.

'Mother, did anyone ever tell you that God loves you?' I enquired.

'I haven't lived to this time of day and don't know that God loves me,' she replied with just the merest touch of indignation.

Carefully weighing my words I continued, 'But do you know that he *so* loved you that he gave his Son for you, as a sacrifice for your sins? A sacrifice which was so sufficient that God brought him back from the dead, a living Saviour. Do you know that you need to make him by faith *your* Saviour?'

Softly she requested, 'Tell me more.'

As I explained the way of salvation God was very near. When I rose to go she gave me one of those bewitching Irish smiles and said, 'Son, I'll never forget this morning.'

That very afternoon I was crossing the moor again. I glanced across at her cottage and there she was, leaning over the half door. I waved and she beckoned me. As I ran up to the door I could see that there were tears in her eyes, but they were tears of joy.

'I've met the Saviour and I'm saved, praise God,' she said.

'Mother, is it really true?' I asked.

'Yes, indeed,' she replied. 'But I have a problem. My daughter is a nursing sister in Belfast and she's coming home in an hour's time. She is a devout Roman Catholic and although I intend to witness that Christ is mine I'm sure she won't understand and there may be trouble.'

'I'll hang around on the moor,' I assured her. 'When I see her arrive I'll come over and try to smooth the path for you.'

I wandered out on the moor. I had time to kill now and I began to look with a slight interest at the natural world around me. Beetles crawled on the ground in front of me, spiders were spinning their webs in the heather and a few day-flying moths hurried by. But none of these held my attention. What interested me more were the plants. You may remember that I had been employed a few years previously at a nursery and whilst there had worked with rockery plants. Had I but known it, there were interesting alpines in the Blue Hills above, but it was fortunate that I was blissfully ignorant of this. Otherwise I might have been tempted to climb up after them and so miss my appointment with the nursing sister. As it was, I wandered up and down on the lower ground looking at the little blue milkwort, the yellow-starred tormentil and the white carpet of heath bedstraw growing bravely under the strong stems of the heather. In a wet hollow I came upon plumes of cotton-grass whispering in the wind and all around these was a thick, rolled out rug of emerald green sphagnum moss. I knew that if I wanted to keep my feet dry I must not go any farther, so I retraced my steps and as I lifted my eyes there was the old lady's daughter approaching the cottage.

I gave her a little while with her mother and then moved towards the cottage not at all sure what I should say. But as I walked I prayed for help. When I got within 100 yards the door opened and the daughter came running out.

'Are you the man who told my mother about the Saviour?' she asked breathlessly. Then she staggered me. She threw her arms around me, kissed me again and again saying, 'I found the Saviour last week in a tent mission. I was afraid to come home and confess it but when I entered the house just now in fear and trembling mother told me that she was saved.'

How good is the God we adore. Was it only my Celtic imagination, or were the flowers on the gorse bushes a deeper, richer yellow than they were a few minutes before?

Almost a Suicide

I looked down from the platform on to serried rows of happy faces, mouths wide-open in full-throated song. The atmosphere would have satisfied any preacher – wonderfully warm, eagerly expectant, spiritually alive. The place was Castlereagh Baptist Church, Belfast, where I was conducting a two week series of Gospel meetings. It was the start of the second week and that night I was particularly pleased with the singing; the congregation were excelling themselves. The joyful sounds of the hymn before my address burst out of the building and were wafted into the street to a dejected figure walking forlornly by.

The singing progressed to the last verse. It was then that from my vantage point I saw the door stealthily open and a bearded man, with distraught face, standing staring up the aisle. He appeared to be a down-and-out, and I ought to be able to recognise one of those! For a moment he was nonplussed for there was not a vacant seat in the church. Then a deacon rose and gave him his own seat. The late-comer looked exceedingly uncomfortable. He hardly knew why he was there. It was certainly not his intention when he set out that night, but the fiery fervour of the singing had drawn him in.

So much had gone wrong with his life. Sin had robbed him of a good job, all his money, his friends, his home. There seemed no way back. 'Better end it all' was his bitter thought. The more he considered the matter the more it seemed the only possible solution. Less than a quarter of a mile from the church flowed the river Lagan, dark and sullen. It was well able to sweep swiftly away to oblivion any human flotsam and jetsam. 'That's it,' he had thought and promptly wrote a note to leave in his overcoat on the bank.

My voice, ringing out, jerked him back to his surroundings.

I was preaching on Naaman, captain of the host of Syria – a capable, likeable, honourable yet miserable character. In many ways I was describing the bearded, despairing man in front of me. For he was no down-and-out, as I had mistakenly surmised, but a gentleman of character until sin had taken over his life. As I spoke about the leper, God spoke to him and he realised that another river than the Lagan held the answer to his problems. Just as Naaman was cleansed in the river Jordan so for him, tainted with the leprosy of sin, 'grace was flowing like a river'. That night he found Christ.

But wait, that is only the beginning. He paid his debts, went to the Irish Baptist College, became pastor of one of the oldest churches in Belfast where he exercised a fruitful ministry. It was my privilege subsequently to preach at the opening of his new church building. Hallelujah! What a Saviour!

The Girl from the Bolshoi Ballet

It was a bitterly cold winter's day as I sat alone in the Bible School office, engaged in my favourite occupation, studying the Word. The scene outside the window was drab and dreary for the leafless hedgerows and trees imparted a sense of desolation to the landscape. The bleakness was heightened by the loneliness of this spot on the crest of the Red Hills, miles from town or village, The lane that leads to the School is narrow and overgrown; scarcely anyone knows to where it leads so that we never have visitors.

As the evening shadows began to fall I felt vaguely apprehensive. Added to the sense of isolation was the knowledge that many tragic, mysterious shootings are bedevilling the Ulster countryside in these troubled times. Friends have often urged me to lock the gate at the end of the lane; whether it is because of a stubborn streak in me that does not take kindly even to well-intentioned advice or just that it is too much trouble, I don't know, but I seldom bother to do so.

Suddenly, footsteps sounded outside. In a flash I was out on the veranda. Perhaps the dividing line between fear and courage is very thin. I couldn't claim to feel courageous – my fast thudding heartbeats would have shouted their denials if I had – but if there was going to be trouble I instinctively felt that I wanted to face it squarely in the open, not like a rat in a trap.

Two total strangers confronted me, a man and a very beautiful young girl.

'Villy Mooland?' the man enquired.

'Yes Sir?' I replied questioningly.

'We are Russians,' he continued. 'My daughter is from the Bolshoi Ballet.'

'Come on in out of the cold,' I interrupted.

It seemed the hospitable thing to do, but I was very wary for I still felt in danger. I looked searchingly at them and watched their every move. I soon discovered to my great relief that my fears were groundless. It was a wonderful story that they had to tell. Six months previously the girl had flown to London with the Bolshoi and whilst there someone had given her the story of my conversion to read. Night after night she read it, then one night she got out of bed, knelt down, committed her life to the Saviour and knew in her heart that she was found of Christ.

Her father wanted to see her perform in the Ballet and after some initial difficulty in obtaining an exit visa he arrived in London the day after her conversion. Like all recently born-again people she was eager to share her new-found faith and was soon pressing my booklet into his hands. He read it thoroughly, studying and marking it and after he had finished, he too gave his life to the Saviour.

They never returned to Russia. Increasingly there grew in them the desire to meet the man who had at long range helped them to Christ and here at last they were, looking into my face. We hugged each other and rejoiced together and then the young woman opened a parcel she was carrying. In it was one of the most beautiful garments I have ever seen. It was her walking-out Russian cape, scarlet in colour, trimmed with fur and bearing elegant fastenings. She asked me to take it as a memento. It hangs in the office now, telling its own wonderful story of God's redeeming grace.

Big MacDowell

I had been invited to conduct a mission at the little town of Dromara in County Down. The meetings were being held in the Baptist church situated a quarter of a mile outside the town. The services had been going for four days and the next morning I decided to stroll into the town. It was winter time, sleet was falling and it was bitterly cold. I turned a corner into the square and bumped into a man. When I say a man, I mean a giant. He was one of the biggest men I have ever seen. On this arctic day he was hatless, wore no vest and his shirt, open to the waist, was flying in the wind. His matted, uncombed hair added to his unkempt and unsavoury appearance.

As I staggered, struggling to keep my balance, I hastily apologised, 'Sure, and I'm sorry.'

A deep, menacing growl was the only reply. He paused for a second, glowered at me and then strode away down the street. When I returned to the good lady who was giving me hospitality for the week I told her of my encounter.

Her eyes opened wide. 'Sure, and that would be Big MacDowell, so it would. Just you keep well out of his way, he's the local ne'er-do-well.'

Little did she know that me being what I am, her kindly concern was likely to have the reverse effect to what she intended. That very afternoon I walked into the town square again. There I found a large crowd of spectators surrounding several horsemen resplendent in scarlet coats and white breeches. Through the onlookers' legs I caught glimpses of a pack of hounds.

I glanced around and there in the middle of the crowd was Big MacDowell. Heedless of my hostess's injunction, or more likely because of it, I shoved my way through the mass of people and marched boldly up to the giant. 'Can you tell me what's going on?' I asked.

He looked down at me for a second or so before answering. 'Why, it's the County Down Stag Hunt,' he said.

'When's it going to start?' I enquired.

'Oh, they'll just be letting off the stag in a minute,' he replied.

'Can I go with you?' I asked.

He glared suspiciously at me and turned to a companion at his side by the name of Simpson. 'Who is this fellow?' he demanded.

'Sure, and it's the preacher at the Baptist meetings, so it is,' he replied.

Big MacDowell gave me a contemptuous look. 'You'd never keep up,' he growled and followed it with a surly laugh.

'You'd never keep up,' echoed Simpson.

'I'd like to try,' I persisted.

Just then the hunt moved off. Most of the crowd remained behind but a few of the hardier and more adventurous followed the horsemen. I tagged on to MacDowell and Simpson who pretended to ignore me but they did not tell me to go away. When the open country was reached the stag was released and bounding away was soon lost to sight. The hounds were soon in full cry.

MacDowell was off like a shot from a gun with Simpson and I closely at his heels. He was over the stone wall at the far side in a bound and we were only just behind. The contest was now on in full earnest and the stag hunt became of secondary significance. This was a trial of physical prowess between Big Mac and me. The field boundaries were not always stone walls. Some were hawthorn hedges and others high banks. I soon noticed that as we crossed the fields each time he headed with deliberate intent for the tallest part of the hedge. Nothing daunted, I followed in reckless abandon. There was the baying of the hounds in front to spur us on and occasionally we caught glimpses in the distance of the hunted stag. Sometimes as we leapt we tumbled over and fell face downwards in the mud but we quickly scrambled up and tore on like madmen. County Down is noted for its hilly countryside and as we ran up and down across the ploughed fields where potatoes had been lifted our hearts were pounding and our breath coming in short gasps.

Many churchgoers would have raised their eyebrows quizzically and looked with pained surprise could they have seen me then. A pastor engaged in the worldly, cruel pursuit of stag hunting? Some, I am sure, would be horrified. I could not have cared less about the stag hunt. I was on a different hunt altogether, a hunt for souls.

Presently Big Mac stopped and said with grudging admiration, 'You're tougher than I thought.'

This was my opportunity which I seized with both hands. 'If I go on to the end will you come to the meeting tonight?' I pleaded.

He hesitated and then said, 'I will if Simpson will.' In the end they both agreed to come.

You should have seen my hostess's face as her mud-encrusted guest returned. A quick bath, a change of clothes, a hurried meal and I was a different man, all ready for the meeting.

Big MacDowell came just as he was and I can tell you, many curious glances were made in his direction. But, after all, are we not told that Jesus was the friend of the outcasts. I preached on the text 'Christ died for the ungodly'. Big Mac began to squirm in his seat, beads of perspiration broke out on his forehead and that night he was gloriously saved. His companion was converted at a later date.

Now the really astonishing, wonderful thing is this. Only two or three weeks later Big MacDowell, the dissolute, the hard drinker and fighter, went to a London Bible college and in due course became minister of a Northern Ireland church. Later he entered into the work of an itinerant evangelist. Does not the wonder of that take your breath away?

The Man in Evening Dress

One Sunday evening I came on the platform to commence a Gospel meeting. The building was packed and I saw a deacon bring in a chair for a very tall, white-haired, distinguished looking man in a dress suit. The congregation consisted in the main of the working and middle classes so that the newcomer stood out like a sore thumb.

I had prepared a sermon on the subject of the Philippian jailer, dealing with the theme of sudden conversions. As the service proceeded I became less sure about the message. The stranger was in my thoughts and I wanted to preach something that would be particularly helpful to him. A text from Daniel came into my mind, 'Thou art weighed in the balances and found wanting.'

While a soloist was singing I carried on a conversation with the Lord. 'Surely you don't want me to preach an unprepared address on this? Why, I don't know much about it and I haven't read the story for sometime.'

Every preacher will, I know, sympathise with me in my dilemma. There is not much that is worse for a preacher than having to make a last-minute sermon switch. But this was worse because I was having to speak quite impromptu and there was the fear that I would trip over my words, or say something that I didn't mean to say, or dry up completely and probably manage all three together. No one likes being made to look a fool in public and I am no exception.

But the Lord's answer was a resounding 'Yes' and I knew the option was being taken from me. So I gave in, 'Lord, if you want to make a fool of me, carry on.' The service now seemed to be flying by and I felt like a canoeist relentlessly being swept towards the rapids. The moment came when all eyes looked expectantly on me; I took a deep breath, squared my shoulders and announced the text – from Daniel! As I began to speak God filled my mind with thoughts. I talked about Judas, Pilate, Lot's wife and others and found a power that was not of me.

After the service was over I went into the vestry and to my surprise I found the man in the dress suit on his knees, crying. I knelt beside him and asked the Lord to help him. We turned and looked at each other whilst still on our knees.

I said, 'You're a stranger here.'

'I've just come back from Australia where I was Inspector of the Constabulary,' he replied. 'The last sermon I heard before I left Ireland forty years ago was on the text you took tonight. I've had material success but my heart is not right with the Lord.'

But it was put right before he left the church that night; he became a member and was exceedingly generous in his monetary gifts to the church. And to think that I almost neglected to obey that inner prompting!

There was another occasion when I felt I was likely to be made to look a fool. I was at Carrickfergus, a town of great antiquity situated on Belfast Lough. The mighty walls of a ruined Norman castle stand on the shoreline. The town was old when Belfast was young and to this ancient town I came with the 'old, old story, of Jesus and his love'.

I was conducting a mission at the Baptist church and, night after night, though I made no appeal, people were being saved. This went on for over two weeks. On the Thursday of the third week I was preaching to a packed church but no one sought salvation that night. An old farmer who lived ten miles away had invited me to have supper with him. I felt strangely reluctant to leave the building but finally walked down the aisle just after nine-thirty p.m. for I saw the caretaker was waiting to lock up.

Outside, my host was waiting. 'It's the first night that nobody has been saved, Willie.'

'Yes, it is, John,' I answered in a pre-occupied way.

As he engaged gear and drove away I felt as though I was being torn from the place where I ought to be. Arriving at the farm we found twenty people already there, gathered for the kind of gargantuan supper that seems to belong especially to farms.

I went into the cloakroom, got down on my knees and prayed. 'Lord, it's after ten o'clock and I can't really explain my feelings to these good folk. They're waiting to start their meal. Can I stop, too, please?'

I have discovered that God doesn't waste time using unnecessary words. 'No,' he said. Terse, clear-cut and very definite.

I called the farmer across to me. 'John, I'm not happy. Can we go back to the church?'

'Why, of course, if you wish. It will be shut up, you know, and no one there,' he answered.

'Never mind, I must go back.'

It was nearly eleven p.m. when we returned to Carrickfergus.

'Where do you want me to take you?' the old man asked.

'Why, straight to the church,' I replied.

There, clinging to the railings like a suffragette, was the kneeling figure of a woman. As I approached I realised that she was crying. I put my hand on her shoulder, 'Are you looking for someone?' I gently enquired.

'Yes,' she answered between her sobs, 'I'm looking for you.' When she calmed down she told me her story.

'I came under conviction of sin tonight but I didn't stop after the meeting. I went home, washed my five children and put them to bed. Then I told my husband that I would have to go back to the church. He said that would be pointless because there would be no one there, but I knew I had to come.'

Sure enough, the doors were shut as her husband had predicted but she was a very determined woman. She knelt on the pavement and in words that reminded me of wrestling Jacob she addressed God, 'I'm not going, Lord, until he comes.'

So I knelt and joined her on the pavement and soon there was joy in heaven. It was a very late supper we had that night but it tasted all the better!

God at the Steering Wheel

The last incident contains an element beyond the rational – a glimpse of supernatural forces outside of our ken. Some might call it a sixth sense, others would say Celtic second sight, dabblers in psychology would label it psychic power, but I, as a plain minister of the Gospel, am content to define it as the guidance of the Lord. It has been experienced by me several times and in some ways it is a disturbing, rather frightening occurrence. I will give you another example. Since pastoral secrets are involved it can only be described in broad outline without the dramatic details.

I happened to be in a certain Irish town one day when two people came up to me in great distress. I took the matter to the Lord in prayer and within a couple of minutes was given the absolute assurance that God was going to solve the prob-

102

lem. We all tumbled into my car, I in the knowledge that the Lord knew where we were going. I'm glad he did, for I certainly didn't! We drove at first along one of the lesser-used roads of the countryside and then the car turned down a narrow lane not much wider than my car. After several miles we turned again down a rough, uneven track which was even narrower. It was lined with dense bushes of bramble which scratched the bodywork of the car. I was literally forcing the car through scrub.

My companions expostulated with me. 'Surely, this can't be right,' they said. 'This doesn't lead anywhere.'

I, myself, didn't particularly want my car damaged but in my heart I knew that this was where we had to go. My hands were sweating with the tension as they grasped the steering wheel, but I continued to drive the car forward. When we came to a wilderness area I pulled up for there, a hundred yards away, was the reason why we had come. Let the Lord's name be praised!

11: Over the water

I believe that the command of Christ to go into all the world and preach the Gospel is a word not restricted to missionaries. After all, the church member on an overseas holiday surely does not cease to be a Christian whilst he is abroad.

My wife and I, however, are stay-at-homes by nature and dislike travel. Mary has never had a holiday in her life, and I have never had any trip which did not involve heavy preaching engagements. Yet when requests came in for me to go overseas, the call to evangelise overcame my inhibitions and I found myself travelling by most forms of transport – car, train, boat, plane and even snow-plough! I have visited the Faeroes, Germany, Greece, Palestine, Syria and Canada. Perhaps you think that these visits are exciting holidays. When I tell you that on a recent tour I preached ninety times in thirty days you will realise that I had precious little time for sun-bathing!

The Irish Sea makes England a country over the water, and one of my early trips was to Liverpool where I addressed a gathering of over 300 women. Travelling with me on this and several other occasions was my friend David Patterson, a wealthy Bangor farmer and business man. He was an exceedingly generous man who had built churches for small, struggling assemblies and wherever he saw the Lord's workers with a need, gave and gave and gave. He was with me on the platform that afternoon just four days before Christmas.

Suddenly he turned and whispered to me, 'How many women are there here?'

I relayed the enquiry to the Chairman, Mrs Ruth Rowland, who after a quick count replied, '304.'

David then descended the platform steps and disappeared. I learnt later that he had dashed to the nearest bank, obtained

1,520 pounds in five-pound notes and handed out one each to the ladies as they left, wishing them a happy Christmas!

He was with me when I went to London and preached at the City Temple. This time, however, his flair for doing the right thing came a little unstuck. He had booked a table at the restaurant at the top of the Post Office Tower. We sat down at the table, the tramp and the millionaire together, and the waitress brought us tea. All very nice, indeed, but soon I became a little uneasy.

'Are you sure we're in the right place?' I asked David.

'Yes, of course, why ever not?'

'Well, then, why are those girls parading at the other end?' I persisted.

He looked in the direction of my eyes and, for the first time since I had known him, looked a little unsure of himself. For the girls wore the elegant clothes and bore the characteristically haughty demeanour of fashion models.

'It's a big fashion show,' he said in a startled voice.

The girls began moving down amongst the tables. It was too late to move without creating a commotion and drawing unwelcome attention to ourselves. We stuck tight.

'This is a right old mess we've got into,' I said cheerfully, 'but we might as well enjoy the show now we're here.'

'But they'll think we're Continental buyers,' he objected.

'Well, we're Irish non-buyers,' I laughed.

It seemed to my bemused eyes that each one made a bee-line for our table. Perhaps that is not a very apt metaphor. They glided smoothly with the suave sophistication that only models possess. I'm sure that to the real buyers present they wore bewitching, enchanting creations but to me they were just dresses and coats. One with a beautiful mink coat paused in front of us and swivelled round so that we might get the complete picture. Well, I was on the lookout for a little present to take back to Mrs Mullan – but perhaps not the mink!

David it was who took Dr Crawford and me on a tour of the Middle East – Athens, Damascus, the Syrian desert, Jerusalem, Samaria, Galilee and the Golan Heights. What a thrill it was for me to preach on Mars Hill at the very place where Paul preached 1900 years ago. It seemed appropriate to speak on the same theme as he did and a large crowd gathered around. Later I was shown around what remained of the glories of the Acropolis. The word means hill or fort and it was this name that I decided to give to my Bible School because it was a spiritual citadel and because it, too, was built on a hill. It was a moving and humble experience also to make a pilgrimage in Israel; to follow in the footsteps of the Master and preach where he did, in Jerusalem, in Samaria and in Galilee.

Another good friend who arranged some meetings outside Ulster was Norman Cordiner, an influential businessman of Aberdeen. I met him by chance, as some might say, at an Easter Conference in the Province, but I prefer to believe that it was providential for that encounter opened up a pathway for me to take the Gospel to some remote islands. Norman had been holidaying in Ireland and dropped in at the conference on Easter Monday. I was the speaker and afterwards he told me that he believed the message was a personal one direct for him.

He became possessed with the idea of getting me over to Aberdeen to tell my life story. He rented the large Music Hall in the city and planned an extensive publicity campaign which ensured that it was filled to capacity with people who came from all over the north of Scotland. Quite astonishingly, a boatload even came through rough seas from the Faeroe Islands far to the north, islands which Scottish fishermen of old used to call the Faraways. That triggered off a desire on the part of the irrepressible Norman to take me on a tour of this remote archipelago. The fact that his own father had once preached there added weight to his desire.

So it came about that one day early in May, 1967, I left Aldergrove airport in Belfast and flew to Aberdeen. As the plane taxied out to the runway a cluster of hares scampered away across the turf. The engines roared into life and soon the hangers and other buildings were little dots below. It was springtime but spring comes late to the Highlands and as we flew over the fertile Vale of Strathmore I could see far to the westward the peaks of the Grampians capped with snow. At

Aberdeen, Norman joined me. I could tell that he was full of excitement and some of this rubbed off on me. The next day saw the second stage of our journey; we flew from Aberdeen to Lerwick. The weather had now made a significant change and as we flew over the North Sea east of Caithness and the Orkneys a dense sea-mist enshrouded the waters below. This of course is an all-too-common phenomenon in these parts and has been for hundreds of years. It was so well known and dreaded by the Viking seafarers that they coined a special word for it – they called it the 'haar'. It is just as much a cause of dread to travellers in the air and I began to wonder if we should be able to land in the Shetlands.

Fortunately it began to lift a little and Sumburgh Head, the southern tip of the Shetland mainland, appeared beneath us. Soon we were circling to land at Lerwick's tiny airfield in the Vale of Tingwall. It was somewhat different from Belfast's busy airport, and that is the understatement of this chapter. There was a shed on one side of the field and a windsock on the other. Unbeknown to me, just before we arrived a shepherd with his collie dog had driven a flock of sheep off the landing strip!

We were to stop overnight at Lerwick and later that day we went sight-seeing around the attractive but exceedingly narrow, cobbled streets above the harbour. We came to the local Baptist church and there to our intense surprise saw a poster which exhorted passers-by to come and hear Willie Mullan that very night! Was this an engagement that Norman had forgotten to tell me about? No, it was only going to be a tape-recording. My sense of fun came to the fore.

'We'll come here tonight, sit quietly at the back and listen to me, so we will,' I said.

'Och, ye'll do nae sich thing,' Norman asserted vigorously. 'Ye'll be giving the address.'

'I certainly shall not,' I retorted.

The matter remained unresolved but as the time of the meeting drew near our footsteps made for the church. It began uneventfully enough but after a little while Norman could contain himself no longer. He rose to his feet and addressed the pastor.

'Ye probably dinna ken, brother, that Willie Mullan himself is sitting beside me and I suggest that ye ask him to speak to us in person,' he said, glancing at me with a triumphant look for which I could cheerfully have floored him! So my speaking engagements began a day early.

If Lerwick's airport is rather primitive, the one at Torshavn, the capital of the Faeroes, is no less so – just a small field on the outskirts of the town from which the boulders of basaltic rock have been removed. There to meet us was Andrew Sloan, the Brethren pastor who was to be our guide and mentor throughout our fortnight's stay and our host for the period we stayed on Streymor, the principal island. He was a sprightly seventy-year-old who had the pastoral oversight of all the islands. His father was the man who began the Brethren work there. We were soon through customs and whisked away to Andrew's home.

The Brethren are the predominant Christian body in the Faeroes although there are a few churches of other denominations including Roman Catholic. Many police officers and Civil Servants are Brethren. A busy round of meetings got under way and hundreds of people crowded into the large Brethren Hall at Torshavn. Of course, I had to have an interpreter and the local schoolmaster, a short, bespectacled man, obliged. I found it a little restricting but on the whole we managed quite well together. I was soon to learn that the Faeroes liked their sermons to be lengthy. Seeing that I am in the habit of preaching for an hour or more at Lurgan, I was happy to oblige. Before I preached Norman would speak for twenty minutes or so, an added bonus for them. Souls were saved, the saints were blessed and the Saviour glorified.

Some of the meetings were held in the open air and my word, the air was extremely cold; I suppose it was not surprising at that latitude, only a few degrees south of the Arctic Circle. There was in fact a strange contrast. The clarity of the light was such that reflection from the snow produced a pronounced glare. So the open-air meetings provided the contradictory spectacle of me wearing both sun glasses and a fur hat which had been presented to me by a Canadian Mountie, and I was heartily glad of both. Not that there was a great deal of sunshine, the dense sea mists were much more in evidence. When British troops were stationed here in the Second World War, with typical sardonic humour they labelled these mists 'Faeroe sunshine'? Although it was the month of May there were still occasional snowstorms. I found that because I was standing still, my feet in particular suffered. One day when they were blue with the cold Andrew Sloan's daughter washed them in warm water and Norman was highly amused, making the inevitable comparison with the biblical incident.

I was too busy preparing and preaching sermons to be able to explore the hills and moors. My only chance to admire the landscape was when we were driven along the narrow roads which seldom ventured far from the coast. It was a quite different environment from the busy, bustling streets of Lurgan. Everything was peaceful and spacious and time seemed almost to stand still. Small bridges crossed streams where stood the ruins of little water mills long since disused. In marshy hollows beside the streams gold kingcups made a splash of colour and above them snipe were 'drumming' in their nuptial display flights. Along the shoreline and in many of the inland fields black and white oystercatchers, the national emblem of the Faeroese, were incessantly piping.

When the tide was out youths could be seen playing football on the beach; it reminded me of my own footballing days but, alas, I no longer had the desire to get out and join them. We passed little groups of men with ropes slung over their shoulders; they were on their way to the cliffs where they would be engaging in the dangerous occupation of collecting birds' eggs for food. Others were busy cultivating the fields, not with ploughs but with small-bladed spades like the ones that were in general use in the Shetlands until recent times.

Some of the roads were quite dangerous. I remember that in one place the road was sited on the edge of a cliff with a sheer 800 feet drop below. The island inhabitants have to learn to live with danger, surrounded as they are by a turbulent sea which is for them a highway. Another kind of hazardous circumstance occurred whilst I was at Vagar, a town on Suderoy which is a large island in the southern group.

A little while before the evening meeting was due to begin, an earthquake took place. Boulders rained down the hillside and many of the folk ran from the town. They ventured back for the meeting, however, and I am glad to say that all was well. It might have tempted publicity agents, had we possessed them, to describe the meetings as earth-shattering events!

Since it was our intention to preach on every inhabited island, much time was spent on the water. Andrew Sloan had laid on for this purpose a large fishing boat with a crew of twenty commanded by Captain Johannsen. The seas were often rough with waves which we estimated to be seventy feet high in the fierce tide races between the islands. Andrew and I were good sailors but the same could not be said for Norman. Whilst we were enjoying ourselves on the bridge Norman was miserably hanging his head over the rails. I took great delight in steering the vessel under the watchful eye of the captain. As we approached our destinations we would often disturb huge rafts of seabirds, especially puffins and guillemots. Sometimes we would sail close to their breeding cliffs and would look up at the serried hordes of birds on their narrow ledges; sometimes a flock of kittiwakes, those lovely little seagulls, would swirl over the boat like giant snowflakes.

At a meeting at Klakksvik, the second largest town in the Faeroes and situated on the island of Bordoy, a bearded man came up to Norman afterwards and told him that he was the best preacher he had ever heard. Now Norman had only spoken for about a couple of minutes! Of course, to tease me he boasted about these remarks, proud as a peacock, until we came to Captain Johannsen's house where we were offered hospitality. There on the wall of the living room was a photo of his crew taken some time earlier and amongst them was this bearded man. On asking the captain about him we learned that he was extremely deaf! We never heard any more from Norman after that!

Most of the time we stayed at Andrew Sloan's house where his wife Annabel plied us with delicious meals. The Faeroese women have a reputation for skilful cooking and they can produce a great variety of unusual dishes such as seabird

110

soup, fish soup, whalemeat, potatoes served with jam and many more. They did not take any chances with me, however, but gave me traditional British meals which, seeing that I have to be very careful with my diet, was perhaps just as well!

When the meal was over twenty or thirty of us would gather together in the large sitting room. Some were seamen, Swedes, Russians and other nationalities as well as Faeroese fishermen. As a consequence much of the casual talk was about fishing. Sometimes the conversations turned to the famous *grindaroo* or whale hunt which happens when a school of ca'ing whales is sighted near the coast. The excitement of these moments is in the blood of the Faeroese and it appears to be a way of life for them.

Although in years long before I had gone out with Mr and Mrs Calder in their boat on fishing trips, I knew nothing about deep sea fishing and I was content to lean back in my chair and listen to the good-natured banter, to Norman cracking his endless jokes and to savour the warmth and depth of fellowship that is only experienced amongst Christians. Often, however, Andrew and Annabel would ask me to continue expounding the Word and so in a very informal way I would give a mini-address and then we would talk together far into the night about the deep things of God. We had turned to consider another kind of fishing – fishing for souls.

We returned home a very long way round by flying to Denmark. There the chief surgeon at a Copenhagen hospital had arranged a meeting for Danish Christians who wanted to hear the story of my life. This was recorded and later translated into Danish. But it is those far-off northern isles which are indelibly printed on my memory. The simple sincerity and warm-hearted friendship of the Faeroese and the ever-open doors of the home of Andrew and Annabel Sloan.

I have paid several visits to Canada. One in particular I shall never forget. Robert Dowie, the Dean of the Bible School at Victoria, New Brunswick had invited me to give a series of addresses at a Spring conference for young people.

As the airliner took off from London airport I settled back

to enjoy the journey. The flight passed uneventfully enough but when we arrived at Montreal in the early hours of the morning, two a.m. to be precise, the pilot startled us by announcing laconically that he was joining his colleagues on a strike! That didn't bother the passengers whose destination was Montreal, but what about those of us who were going farther? In particular, what about me who had to travel 500 miles north-east to New Brunswick. Consternation and dismay registered on our faces, but there was no help forthcoming. Disconsolately, we tumbled out of the aircraft. At first we huddled together in small groups as we discussed our dilemma. One by one the numbers dwindled as individuals wandered off in desperation to seek other forms of transport. No one had any ideas how my problem could be solved and, in any case, I had no Canadian currency whatsoever on me. Soon I was the only passenger left. This airport has the reputation of being one of the busiest in North America but you would not have thought so then! The poet writes of Ruth being sad at heart and sick for home but she did at least have a loving mother-in-law with her. I was really forlorn.

Imagine my feelings! I have mentioned earlier my dislike of travel unless accompanied by a guide and here was I, in the middle of the night, alone and deserted in a foreign country. Well, not quite alone. A solitary Royal Canadian Mountie paced slowly up and down the passenger hall, every now and then eyeing me with what I was convinced was deep suspicion. On reflection, he was probably thinking, 'What's that silly old buffer waiting for, an angel to come?'

And that is what happened, in a manner of speaking. Suddenly the large doors of the hall swung open and a lame man limped towards me. Would you believe it, he said, 'Willie Mullan?' in a questioning voice.

It was a classic Stanley–Livingstone encounter. It turned out that the folk at New Brunswick hearing of the strike had become anxious and put through a long-distance call to a pastor of a Montreal church, Henry Holden by name. He had risen from a sick bed to come and look for me. I spent the rest of the night with him, and the next morning, anxious to do him a good turn, I preached for him as he was clearly not well enough to do so.

So far so good but I was not getting any nearer to my destination. After some enquiries my new-found host ascertained that there was a cattle train travelling to New Brunswick. Attached to the long line of trucks loaded with loudly-protesting cattle was one sleeper van in the charge of a coloured guard. After a moment or two's hesitation, he agreed to take me on board. The lowing of the cattle made me think of those days long ago when I obtained casual work on farms and I was reminded, too, that these were amongst the first sounds that the baby Jesus heard.

Soon we were passing over a drawbridge spanning the great St Lawrence Seaway. The railroad wound eastwards through mountains which are a northern extension of the Appalachian range. They consist of rugged hills, river valleys and dense coniferous forests in which pine and spruce are interspersed with maple. Although it was early spring there had been recent heavy snowfalls and I looked out of the window at a landscape of fairyland. But snow, however beautiful it looks, has distinct disadvantages for travellers as I was soon to discover. After we had journeyed about 200 miles the engine stuck in a mammoth snow drift. We were in a cutting in the mountains. Thick woods of tall spruce surrounded us in which from time to time rustling branches indicated the passage of small groups of white-tailed deer and possibly an occasional moose. For all I knew there might have been bears in that forest, but as I paced aimlessly along the track my thoughts were on other matters.

A growing frustration took hold of me. I hadn't come all this way to admire the scenery or study the habits of the deer. Why had the Lord got me out of one tangle of transport only to land me in another? If we were firmly stuck it did not seem likely that another engine would be any more successful even assuming that one could be sent for. We were well and truly stranded.

It was then that the Lord sent another angel. He came striding along the track in a scarlet jacket and swinging an axe – a real, live Canadian lumberjack.

With a quizzical grin he accosted me, 'Sure, and what would you be doin' on a cattle train?'

Another Ulster man! Hastily I explained my predicament to him and he very generously offered to try and take me 200 miles farther on to St John's Point in New Brunswick. He insisted on carrying my case so in exchange I bore his axe. Reinvigorated now I felt energetic and light-hearted enough to chop a tree down; a load of anxiety had been taken off my mind. After walking along the track for some distance we came to a point where the road met the railway and there on the road was a snowplough. Perched high on the plough I must have looked rather a comical sight but I didn't care about that as long as I was getting to my objective. As we journeyed along we reminisced together over the Ireland that he had known. Slowly but steadily we trundled on to St John's Point where I took a grateful farewell of my fellow Irishman.

The scenery was now distinctly mellower. This was rich agricultural land that grows potatoes in quantity. Many of the inhabitants are evangelical Christians so that the district is sometimes called the Bible Belt, sometimes the Potato Belt. The one common factor seems to be that they are both good, solid food! At the Bible School I was welcomed like the prodigal son for they, not unnaturally, had completely lost track of me in my somewhat unorthodox travels and had become worried over my well-being. But all came out well in the end and I believe that the Lord himself had taken a hand in the transport arrangements.

12: Advance on the home front

I may have unwittingly given the impression in the preceding chapters that much of my time has been spent away from my own church, indeed, from my own land. That, of course, is not the case at all. It is just that the officers of the church have been generous and far-sighted enough to look beyond the needs of their own spiritual community. Their consuming interest is spreading the Gospel wherever the opportunity occurs be it in Lurgan, Belfast or New Brunswick. They have therefore willingly loaned me to other churches as the occasion arose.

But the vast majority of my days in the last twenty-five years have been spent in Lurgan, involved in the solid, if not always spectacular, consolidation and extension of this particular corner of God's vineyard.

Five years after my arrival it was clear that the church was too small, so in 1958 an extension was built which provided accommodation for a further 200 people. We rejoiced at the spiritual surge forward of which the bricks and mortar were the 'outward and visible sign', but of course the work inevitably disrupted the normal pattern of our church life. The Sunday services had to be held in the Town Hall. Early on Sunday mornings a team of willing helpers could be seen converging on the building to set out the chairs after the previous night's festivities.

What a relief it was when we could return to the familiar yet changed surroundings. As well as the extra accommodation the architect had provided a modern kitchen and toilet block. Things were looking up. It is at this stage in a church's life that there looms a great danger. It is all too easy to become inward-looking and self-satisfied as success seems almost self-perpetuating. We were very conscious of this and tried as best we could to keep a wide vision and an outgoing ministry. The Tuesday Bible Class kept us in touch with Christians of other denominations; various members of the congregation entered full-time Christian service and we constantly kept in the forefront of our hearts and minds the call of our Lord to evangelism. We sought to answer that call not only by the regular preaching of the Word but by special campaigns both within the church itself and far beyond.

The self-sacrificial labour of missionaries in spreading the Gospel across the world was a work we were eager to identify ourselves with, and in 1965 one of our elders, Mr William Russell, devised a scheme which he called Missionary Enterprise. In essence it was very simple. It asked people voluntarily to contribute a shilling a week in addition to their other financial contributions to the Lord's work. Each year the sum collected is distributed amongst the various missionary societies at the annual Missionary Conference. To date many thousands of pounds have been collected in this way.

The following year the office bearers of the church approached me with a proposal. The church secretary, Mr Sam Best, was their spokesman.

'We are thinking of having an old-time, old-fashioned Gospel Mission here at the church to seek to evangelise the whole town and neighbourhood,' he said.

I thought it was an excellent idea and was prepared to give it my whole-hearted backing. 'Any idea who the preacher should be?' I enquired.

'Why you, of course, nobody but you,' Mr Best replied.

'In my own church after many years of preaching?' I queried doubtfully.

'Why not?' they chorused.

So since it was evidently their unanimous desire, I agreed to undertake this task. It was plain to all of us from the outset that a great deal of work would be involved – much planning, prayer, preaching and practical work. But it was wonderful that the church was going all out to help men and women find new life in Christ, and that was a tremendous incentive to me as we got down to this mighty business.

One of the first decisions to be made was that no offerings

would be taken at any of the meetings – we would have to meet the expenses ourselves. The next Sunday morning I faced the congregation and did not mince my words.

'If you really desire to carry out this great work for the Lord you must be prepared to put your money where your heart is. Every man or woman (pensioners and young people excepted), who can give twenty pounds let them bring it and lay it on the vestry table tonight.' With these words I challenged them.

That evening we had over three thousand pounds, our money problems had been solved at a stroke and many a heart gave God the glory that night. The next day the fourteen leaders met together for a long session of prayer and very careful preparation. It was decided that we should run this campaign for three weeks which would involve the preaching of twenty-one Gospel messages. I was advised to concentrate exclusively on the message and not be available for anything else. This was clearly essential. No visiting, no phone calls, no nothing! And that's how it was. From five o'clock in the morning until the time of the evening meeting I drew near to God and he drew near to me. In the process the messages came with unfailing regularity.

There was much more to arrange. A man was appointed to organise transport, in particular to impress on all car owners to make sure that all their seats were filled each night. Another official appointment was that of publicity manager, who for two weeks prior to the start took over the centre pages of our local newspaper. Then we asked each member of the congregation to take at least one soul upon their hearts, pray for them and bring them by hook or by crook to the meetings. From the youngest to the oldest they responded magnificently.

In confident faith we believed that our own building would not be large enough to accommodate the crowds so we leased an adjacent disused linen factory and installed closed circuit television. It was a good job we did for 1,400 people packed the two buildings each night and our faith was abundantly justified. We had the Woodvale Male Quintet, the Richardson Sisters and Fay O'Brien to sing each evening. I preached

117

God's message nightly and, although I made no appeals and used no pressure, both Protestant and Catholic men and women broke down in tears and passed from death to life eternal.

It was partly as a result of this mission that three years later it was decided to purchase the disused factory; after it was partitioned into separate classrooms it became the Sunday school which comprises about two hundred scholars and twenty teachers.

As any healthy church should, the growing membership at Lurgan contained a number of fine young men with latent preaching ability. But their skills had to be developed and in particular their knowledge of biblical doctrines had to be extended. Over a period I was much exercised in my mind about this and in spare moments pondered the possibility of having a Bible School. My time as a tramp ensured that I never had the slightest difficulty in waking up before daybreak, and in the early mornings I used to take the matter to the Lord in prayer. I soon realised that a considerable sum of money would be needed to buy the land and erect the buildings. Whilst I was quite prepared to plough in what money I had for this project, which was now becoming an obsession with me, I could not see this being elastic enough to stretch as far as would be required.

This matter was still relentlessly turning over and over in my mind as I approached the farm of Jim Morrow of Taughlomney. The land around Lurgan, south-east of Lough Neagh, is fertile, watered by the rivers Lagan and Bann and by a copious supply from the heavens. Jim, a member of the church, had a well-run beef-producing farm where he and his wife Phyllis were the only workers. This entailed working from daylight to dark throughout the week with a few hours' essential work thrown in on Sundays. Despite the hard toil he was a happy and successful man for he kept his big Bible on the breakfast table and talked over the details of the day's work with the Lord. No wonder it was a success story all the way. In all his undertakings he was fully supported by his loyal and devoted wife.

Jim welcomed me that day with his usual hospitable

welcome and later as we were walking the fields together I told him of the pipe-dream that lay uppermost in my mind and heart.

He listened intently as I waxed eloquent over my ambitions and then enthusiastically responded, 'Look! Here is a whole farm – many acres. The Lord can have what he wants, where he wants and when he wants. Free, absolutely free. What's more,' he continued, bringing me down to earth with a bump, 'you and I will build it ourselves.'

I was dumbfounded – on two counts. All my anxious concern had been unnecessary; Jim's generosity took my breath away. His bold proposition that we should do all the work ourselves also rendered me speechless, for a totally different reason. Did either of us have the necessary skills and the time? I soon recovered. Jim must be experienced in putting up sheds and I, who was no stranger to hard manual work, could be his labourer.

My restored enthusiasm moderated again when Jim said, 'You'll have to draw the plans.'

I had never drawn building plans before and this would be a sizeable structure with one of the rooms needing to seat 100 students. I soon perked up. The Lord was obviously behind us, he would see me through.

The provision of an adequate supply of water was a vital necessity at an early stage and here my friend Ian Paisley came to my assistance. One of his little-known gifts is the mysterious art of water-dowsing. Holding a rod between his two outstretched hands he paced up and down the land until suddenly the rod almost leapt from his hands – he had located the site for the well.

It was not long before Jim and I were enthusiastically digging the trenches for the foundations. One morning shortly afterwards the lorry carrying the ready-mixed concrete arrived. As it stood at the site the steady but relentless revolutions of its huge tank seemed to symbolise our own unflagging determination to let no obstacle stand in our way. By evening the foundations were complete.

The next target was the walls and work proceeded apace. Jim was the mason and I was merely the labourer. He was a tireless worker and kept me continually on the go whilst I was there. Of course, I had to remind myself that I was also a pastor and often I had to leave the site to carry out some church duties. When this happened I had to work doubly hard to pile up a huge heap of concrete blocks ready for his use. Then I would change my old dusty clothes and dash off to the hospital or maybe visit some troubled soul at home. When I returned, Old Faithful would still be hard at work.

There is a corny old joke amongst non-churchgoers that the sermons of the clergy send the congregation to sleep. Well, as I mixed the cement I used to preach next Sunday morning's message to Jim and sometimes I confess I used wistfully to wish that it might have a mildly soporific effect on him. But did it? Not on your life! It seemed to act as a stimulant rather than a sedative and above the noise of the trowel I could often hear the words 'Praise the Lord!'

One morning whilst we were at work something quite extraordinary and wonderful happened. A large, imposing-looking car drew up at the site and out stepped a Belfast businessman, head of a famous firm of building contractors. He was Mr Bertie Scott, an old friend of mine. How the news reached him I shall never know but perhaps it was carried by the wind as it whispered through the green grass of our Emerald Isle. He looked at the preacher and the farmer, threw back his head and roared with laughter. For maybe a fraction of a second I felt a little sheepish, then came the realisation that I was proud of our efforts. 'I'll show him' I thought as I squared my shoulders, stuck my chin jauntily in the air and gave the newcomer a personally conducted tour of the shell of the Bible School.

He scrutinised everything with great care including the plans and finally enquired dubiously, 'Willie, do you really think that you and Jim can do this?'

'We don't think it, we're sure of it,' I replied with what I thought was a splendid gesture of proud defiance.

Bertie remained totally unimpressed. Perhaps his thoughts were on the story in the good book of the man who made an abortive attempt to build a tower and was not able to finish it. It was certainly no good him quoting the parable of the foolish man who built his house on the sand for there was nothing wrong with our foundations, at any rate.

He made a decisive movement. 'Willie,' he said, 'I'm taking over here from this moment. Tomorrow morning I will send a lorry with a foreman and a gang of men. I will have the large plate glass windows cut in the workshop and we have all the material available for the roof and this great veranda of yours. I want to put your mind at rest,' he continued, 'I'm doing this for the Lord and it won't cost you anything.'

When he had gone, Jim and I looked at each other. 'Praise the Lord,' said Jim.

True to his word, Bertie Scott completed the work that we had just begun. In addition, for good measure, he designed and built a big office adjacent to the School which has been extremely useful to me. I am never likely to forget the opening day of the Acropolis Bible School, as we called it. The big classroom was packed with students and it was a joy to see Bertie Scott's smiling face as he sat surrounded by young preachers in the making. Jim Morrow was too shy and self-effacing to come in for he regarded himself as a backroom boy. What a boy! I can tell you one thing – there were no prouder men in the whole of Armagh that day than those two big-hearted men.

About thirty students at a time attend every weekend on a three year course. They can be of any age. What of the students who were present that day? Well, some today are pastors, some are on the mission field in Brazil, Chile and Ethiopia whilst others are evangelists in the Province. Two of these have held tremendous meetings full of spiritual power in the border country between North and South in an area known, not without good reason, as the Murder Triangle. There for three weeks in a place where angels might fear to tread they preached the Gospel to large crowds every night and many came to know Jesus as a personal Saviour. How proud and pleased I was to be able to support them on two nights of the campaign.

The Bible School today with its gleaming white walls is considered to be one of the lovely buildings of the Ulster countryside and it is well-maintained. We are fortunate indeed in having as members of the church a number of men connected in one way or another with the building industry, all of whom take a pride in voluntarily keeping the building ship-shape. Right from the start I always felt that God was really for us in this thing. The ground was free, the building materials and labour were free, the heating and lighting is still free. I have lectured hundreds of times and spent thousands of hours there and I trust that God has enabled me to help scores of young preachers. I have never asked a student for a penny and never will. No! This was all of God and therefore all must be for God.

Any church with a large congregation is bound to have a great variety of talents amongst its members. Few are more valuable to the pastor personally than highly proficient secretarial skills. Certainly, that is true for me and I suspect for most of my brothers in the ministry. Sermon preparation, devotions, meetings, pastoral visits and the business aspects of a church's life leave little enough time for dealing with correspondence and keeping papers tidy. Especially is this true if that side of things holds no appeal, anyway!

Some considerable time ago, a young lady came to see me in some distress because of deep spiritual trouble. As she told me her story I soon realised that her problems were real and difficult. I turned to the Lord for guidance and by his grace I was enabled to show her what God's will was for her. She followed the path that God had opened up for her and in doing this she found joy and peace.

Her name is Miss Irene Campbell and she is secretary to the Professor of Chemistry at Queens University, Belfast. In due course she and her brother joined the church at Lurgan. She immediately put her considerable gifts at our disposal. The duplicating of 600 copies of Bible notes each week was no light task but her work did not end there. She took down in shorthand the Sunday morning messages and made them into attractive booklets which were sent all over the world. Not content with this, she next turned her attention to the onerous burden of classifying twenty-five years of sermon notes and placing them into a number of large leather bound volumes. I once did a series of one-and-a-half-hour lectures

122

for fourteen weeks on the tribes of Israel; later I did several more series on a variety of subjects. All of these talks she took down word for word and compiled them into beautifully presented bound volumes. When I pause to think about it I wonder however she has been able to do so much work. She eats up work as a starving man consumes a loaf of bread. Secretarial talent seems to run in the family for her very capable brother is now the secretary of our church.

By 1973 I had been twenty years at Lurgan and to celebrate my anniversary Irene wrote in verse the story of my life, which she entitled 'A Shepherd of the Sheep'. Before me as I write I have this brochure with its bright, evocative cover portraying sheep in the green fields of Ulster. The words of Jesus are indeed true – 'Give and it shall be given unto you; good measure, pressed down . . . running over . . . ' The help that I was able to render has rebounded on me in abundance.

1978 found me still at Lurgan in the twenty-sixth year of my ministry there. I now have four assistant ministers to undertake the pastoral work; two of them do the visiting in the country districts, the other two call on the sick in the town and pay daily visits to the hospitals. I have been forcefully reminded that time does not stand still and have had to reduce my commitments to the preparation and preaching of no more than four new sermons each week, which some kindly folk tell me is still too much. The church has very generously made a present of the manse to my wife and me and this will mean that we shall have no house-hunting worries when the time comes to retire.

Meanwhile preaching is a labour of love to me and so long as I have the health to do this I want to continue. For the last fifteen years I have taken the Bible readings and exposition at the great Convention in Portrush in early August. This is followed by the annual conference of the Christian Police Association of which I am the honorary padre. Perhaps it strikes you as very funny that an ex-criminal should be chaplain to the police. But don't you think that the Lord has a sense of humour? I do. There is, in any case, a precedent. Fred Lemon, who tells his life story in *Breakout*, is an ex-prisoner from the East End of London who has long been an active member of his local branch of the CPA.

I still conduct the occasional mission and have recently completed a quite extraordinary campaign at the Iron Hall, Belfast, during the month of November, 1978. It has been described, not without justification, as the Battle for Bally-macarrett. This is the district in East Belfast in which the Iron Hall is situated. The shipyard is nearby and many tough, rough men live in the neighbourhood. The Iron Hall itself has long been a kind of cathedral for evangelical truth.

It was many months ago that the overseers of this assembly invited me to be the preacher and began an extremely thorough and detailed preparation for this event which they were assured was under the guidance of God. They did not underestimate the importance of precise, practical details. It was both sound common sense and courtesy on their part to notify local churches at an early date so that as far as possible dates would not clash. Publicity was chiefly by a four-page leaflet which was distributed to every home in the area by a team of fifty workers. In addition, other members went in small groups to local organisations to announce the event and make arrangements for the members to come as a group to the meetings. One small team specialised in visiting public houses whilst the campaign was under way and this proved to be fruitful work. Also during the mission several cars fitted with loud-speakers constantly toured the district. Transport was effected by many cars and by mini-buses, some of which were borrowed from local churches. The whole operation was controlled in a modern way by two-way radio.

The most significant factor in the success of the mission, however, was the intensive spiritual preparation which was made. Throwing themselves into the practical work the members found their enthusiasm for the spiritual aspect quickened. The assembly includes many talented people – preachers, singers, instrumentalists. These frequently give their services to other churches but during the approach and throughout the mission their rich gifts were available to their own assembly. A united choir of sixty voices spent long hours in rehearsal and contributed much blessing. On twelve Sundays beforehand a series of addressses was given by the

124

pastor on the subject of revival. A team of counsellors was trained to give guidance to the seeking souls that were confidently expected. A great deal of evangelistic work was undertaken by the Young People's Fellowship before the mission proper began. About 100 teenagers held open-air services in the streets of the neighbourhood on several Saturday afternoons. Before they went out they met for a time of prayer.

I myself am convinced that what happened at the mission was overwhelmingly due to the praying pastor and people of the Iron Hall assembly. For it was not only the teenagers who prayed. No, the women of the assembly also held prayer meetings in the Hall but the big event was the daily meeting for prayer of the congregation during the three weeks prior to the campaign and during the campaign itself. It was scheduled for seven a.m. to nine a.m. each day but in fact almost invariably began at six-thirty a.m. These early morning prayers were periods when rich blessings fell from heaven. I am told that one member who had only himself been a Christian for less than two years expressed his astonishment in his prayer.

'Lord, whatever's happening? Every day is like Christmas!'

With that great volume of prayer it is not surprising that souls were saved before the campaign even began and continued after it had ended. So the mission began. Each day from six-thirty a.m. to six-thirty p.m. I spent with the Lord. I had brought nothing with me but just passed on the message which God gave me each day. Each evening folk broke down and came into the enquiry rooms. Some of the toughest men you could possibly meet were gloriously saved. One such was Ted, a big man of about 19 stone and 6′ 4″ high. A tough man if ever there was one. As soon as he came into the vestry he fell to the floor sobbing. He confessed sins of an enormity which would make you tremble but that night he laid down his arms of rebellion against his maker.

The next day he was at the early morning prayer meeting. The pastor, Jack Mitchell, led the first prayer. He was followed by a young man who prayed for his family. Then Ted tugged nervously at his tie. 'I'm a changed man,' he said,

'I can't pray like you people but I need to pray for this district now.' So he prayed, in his own words and in his own way. As he prayed the whole meeting broke down and wept tears of joy.

Another convert was an elderly man who had spent forty years of his life in prison. Now his chains had fallen off and he was spiritually as well as physically free. Teenagers who had gone astray were reconciled both to God and to their parents who yearned for them and who had so often prayed for their salvation. Who can describe the abundant happiness which came to these families? We who were present could only marvel and feel a lump rising in our own throats. In all, about 120 people entered the Kingdom during the fortnight. The remarkable fact was that they were of all ages and from many varied conditions. The poor and the wealthy knelt side by side; criminals and policemen together; Roman Catholics and Protestants hugged each other. Jesus, the great Reconciler was present and active amongst his people. At a conservative estimate 900 people attended each night. On the final night crowds began gathering two and a half hours before the commencement. An hour later a long queue had formed stretching right down the street. It was necessary to open the doors early and bring the starting time forward. The 600 seats in the church itself rapidly filled and so did the overflow room with its closed circuit television and accommodation for a further 250; next 50 chairs were placed in the entrance hall and more down the aisles; then the counselling rooms, vestry, even the kitchen and cloakrooms were pressed into service but still hundreds of people regretfully had to be turned away.

I think I may have mentioned in an earlier chapter that I do not like using the word 'revival', but I have been forced to admit that this was a kind of revival in the east end of Belfast. The outstanding fact was that God's hand was manifestly on the whole affair; he was in the organising; in the singing; in the praying; in everything that was done. It was impossible not to be aware of his presence amongst us. I have been involved in many missions but never one like this. To his blessed name I give all the glory and all the praise.

Epilogue

The problem of writing one's own life story is that it is inevitably mainly 'I'. I want to end this account of my chequered career by turning your thoughts away from myself to our precious Saviour.

When I was a young man of about thirty years of age I sat in my study early on Christmas day completing the finishing touches to a sermon that I was to preach later that morning. That done, a creative calm descended on me and the poetic muse hovered over my head. I am certainly no poet, but these words just arrived and I wrote them down as quickly as I could:

> *God manifest in flesh, oh wonder to behold!*
> *Creative power within the breast that felt the blast of cold.*
> *God in our likeness made, oh may we understand*
> *The One who made the wondering worlds appear as lowly*
>   *man!*
> *He stood within the realm He fashioned with a thought;*
> *His creatures gazed upon Him; alas they knew Him not,*
> *They cried out for His blood, His claims cast down as dross,*
> *They spat upon His princely face, then nailed Him to a cross.*
> *BUT He made the tree for that cross of wood,*
> *He made the hill on which it stood,*
> *And in some hidden vein of land*
> *He made the steel that pierced each hand;*
> *He made the sun which hid its face;*
> *He made the fathers of that race*
> *Who, in their hatred knew Him not.*
> *He made the fiends with which He fought,*
> *And there, in death, He made a way*
> *Back to Himself*
> *Eternally.*

Also available in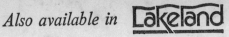

BREAKOUT

Fred Lemon with Gladys Knowlton

It was very quiet in my cell after the warder had escorted me back from the 'dungeons' – the punishment cells. I threw myself on the hard bed, a black bitterness of soul filling me. Tomorrow, I vowed, I would get hold of the sharpest knife in the mailbag room – and there would be murder done. Weary and tormented I pulled the coarse blanket round my shoulders and closed my eyes.

Something made me sit up suddenly. There were three men in the cell with me; they were dressed in ordinary civvy suits. The man on the right spoke:

'Fred,' he said, 'This is Jesus . . . '

Fred Lemon, a confessed criminal, on the eve of attempting to break out of Dartmoor, unexpectedly broke out spiritually, and found this freedom far greater than that of the open moor.

This story of an East End child who grows into a violent criminal, simply and powerfully shows how criminality breeds and takes a man step by step into the abandonment of hell, and yet how Christ can meet a man even there.

GOING STRAIGHT

Fred Lemon with Gladys Knowlton

In this book Fred invites you to come and share some of his experiences since the prison gates clanged behind him. He says, 'You will find in these pages that even the most ordinary setting – a shop, a homely room – can become the place where miracles take place, and that extraordinary things can happen to the most ordinary people.'